A *Fresh Look* at the
Our Father

REDISCOVERING THE POWER
OF THE LORD'S PRAYER

David M. Knight

TWENTY-THIRD PUBLICATIONS
twentythirdpublications.com

TWENTY-THIRD PUBLICATIONS
One Montauk Avenue, Suite 200
New London, CT 06320
(860) 437-3012 or (800) 321-0411
www.twentythirdpublications.com

Cover photo: ©AdobeStock / Matteo Girelli

ISBN: 978-1-62785-676-8
Printed in the U.S.A.

 A Division of Bayard, Inc.
Bayard CEO: Hugues de Foucauld

CONTENTS

INTRODUCTION

"A Summary of the Whole Gospel"

TERTULLIAN, *DE ORATIONE* 1

As I began my ninetieth year as a Catholic and sixtieth as a priest, I was asked to teach a comprehensive religion course to the novices of the Poor Clare monastery in Huehuetenango, Guatemala.

I saw this as a call to gather together a rich life—almost a hundred years of Catholic living—and condense it all into a few conferences that would sum up everything I have learned about what it means to live as a Christian. A daunting task, but an exciting one! What I found is that everything essential is already summarized in the prayer taught by Jesus himself, the Our Father.

Don't take my word for this. Tertullian said, "The Lord's Prayer is truly the summary of the whole gospel." St. Augustine agreed: "Run through all the words of the holy prayers [in Scripture], and I do not think that you will find anything in them that is not contained and included in the Lord's Prayer." St. Thomas Aquinas added, "The Lord's Prayer is the most perfect of prayers....In it we ask, not only for all the things we can rightly desire, but also...in what order we should desire them" (see *Catechism of the Catholic Church*, 2761–63).

Jesus originally taught the Our Father as an answer to his disciples' request: "Lord, teach us to pray" (Luke 11:1). What he taught them was not a formula of words to be memorized, or even a method of prayer, but a list of things to pray for: what Jesus himself prayed for, lived for, and died for. Effectively, he was saying, *If you make my priorities your priorities in your prayer and in your life, you will learn how to pray. And how to live.*

Jesus knew that the more we ask God for something, the more we will grow to desire it. So the Our Father is a way to form our hearts to become like the heart of Jesus, longing and living for what he longed and lived for.

But see for yourself. Take a slow look at the Our Father, asking yourself how wonderful it would be if all it asks for were realized in your life—and throughout the world.

How to Begin

"Christ in you, the hope of glory" COLOSSIANS 1:27

Never just get out of bed in the morning. *Rise up* to live a life filled with joy, enthusiasm, and purpose. Jesus Christ is rising from the dead in you. You are his body. He is going to live this day *with you, in you,* and *through you.* Rise up to be *immersed in Christ*!

Rise up to swirl with the Three Persons in the dance of divinity. Rise up to "be God" by sharing in the divine life of Father, Son, and Spirit. By baptism you "became Christ" (*Catechism of the Catholic Church*, 795). Rise up to live the mystery of your being, "the grace of the Lord Jesus Christ," by which you live "in Christ" and Christ in you.

Then go out to live your day. As the Father sent Jesus, so Jesus sends you—to bear fruit that will enhance lives forever.

Praying the Our Father will get you started. It is a prayer to be absorbed, to recite reflectively and affectively. It is a prayer to enter into, in which to lose and find ourselves. It is "the Lord's prayer," the prayer of Jesus himself, meant to focus us on being like Jesus himself.

When we pray the Our Father, we want to take care not just to say the words, paying more attention to getting them said than to absorbing what we are saying. Instead, we want to ingest them like "sippin' whiskey," tasting each word, rolling it around in our heads, taking it into our hearts. When we really pray the prayers we say, truth travels from mouth to head to heart.

This way of saying prayers, stopping to taste every word, letting every thought sink in, is a way to pass from saying prayers to praying what we say.

Let us put this into practice now and, like Mary (see Luke 2:19), treasure all these words and ponder them in our hearts.

Part One

AWARENESS OF RELATIONSHIP

Our Father, who art in heaven

"When you pray, say: 'Father'..."

See what love the Father has given us, that we should be called children of God; and that is what we are. 1 JOHN 3:1

One of the most exciting things about Christianity is that by teaching us to pray "*Father*" Jesus redefined religion as *relationship*. He tells us the focus of our religion should not be on worship, obedience, service, or even adoration of God. All of these are essential. But they are not the most important, nor do they characterize our religion. What characterizes our religion is *relationship*.

Think what it means that Jesus tells us to call God "Father." That overwrites every other way of relating to God—for example, as Creator, Lawgiver, Judge, even as God. In the Gloria at Mass "Father" is the title we build up to: "Lord God, heavenly King, O God, almighty *Father*."

Jesus tells us that when we come before God in prayer, that most important of encounters, what we should be most aware of is this family relationship. *"When you pray, say: 'Father'...."* God is no longer just our Creator. We are no longer just creatures. God has become our Father by sharing with us God's own divine life. Infinite life. God has made us divine.

The first thing Jesus wants us to appreciate is this mystery that erases the distance that separates us. We have the right to call God "Father," a right that is not to be taken for granted. We introduce the Our Father at Mass with the words, "We *dare* to say: *Our Father....*" We take it for granted only because it is granted.

This is unique to Christianity. Christians alone can explain how we are related to God as family. God doesn't just treat us that way; now God actually is our true Father. By baptism we have been born a second time, reborn of water and Spirit (John 3:5) as sons and daughters of the Father. That makes us God's family. And that makes us divine.

Everything in our religion should be based, and focused, on this new relationship and on all the relationships it entails: relationship with Jesus, not only as disciples, or even as friends, but as his brothers and sisters and as living members of his body on earth. Relationship with the Spirit whom God has sent into our hearts, bearing witness with our spirit when we cry, "Abba! Father!" that we are children of God (Galatians 4:6; Romans 8:15–16). Relationship with other humans as our brothers and sisters "in Christ." Relationship with the universe as responsible "stewards of creation."

We need to begin every day trying to absorb this a little more. If we wake up praying *"Our Father, who art in heaven...,"* we begin our day consciously entering into the mystery of our all-transforming relationship with God and others. We enter into the mystery of who we are. We see ourselves now not just as creatures but as God's own sons and daughters. As divine.

This is Christianity. Our religion is a conscious relationship with God as "*Our Father in heaven.*" That is the first thing Jesus wants us to learn: "When you pray, say: '*Father*'...."

We "*Become God!*"

(St. Basil the Great)

We mustn't overlook the logical implication of being true children of the Father: we are *divine.* That is an inescapable conclusion. Like Father, like child. If God is our Father, we are not just God's creatures but God's children. And children are what their parents are. If our father is human, we are human. If our Father is God, we have to say we are God. We share in, and live by, the infinite, eternal life of God. This is our identity. This is what it means to be a *Christian.*

We don't think of ourselves this way. It shocks us to hear St. Athanasius (c. AD 296–373) say the Word was "made human so that we might be *made God*" (*On the Incarnation* 54.3). St. Basil the Great (AD 329–379) writes: "Through the Spirit we acquire a likeness to God; indeed...we *become God*!" (Office of Readings, Tuesday, Seventh Week of Eastertide). As a result, the Trappist monk Michael Casey writes in his book *Fully Human, Fully Divine*: "According to the teaching of many Church Fathers, particularly those of the East, *Christian life consists not so much in being good as in becoming God.*"

St. Augustine is just as shocking. He says to the baptized, "Let us rejoice then and give thanks that we have become not only Christians but *Christ himself.* Do you understand and grasp, brothers and sisters, God's grace toward us? Marvel and rejoice: we have *become Christ*" (quoted in the *Catechism of the Catholic Church*, 795).

For God to be our Father, we have to be God's children. But God has only one natural child, God the Son, Jesus, the "only begotten Son of the Father." So the only way for us to be true children of the Father is for us to be sons and daughters "in the Son." We share in God's life by being incorporated into the body of Jesus at baptism. We are living in Christ; Christ is living in us.

That is who we are. Christians are those who, by mystically dying and rising in Christ, have become a *new creation*. "If anyone is *in Christ*, there is a new creation: everything old has passed away; see, everything has become new!" (Galatians 2:20; 2 Corinthians 5:17).

Mass usually begins, "The grace of the Lord Jesus Christ...be with you." "Grace" means the gift, the favor, of sharing in the divine life of God. Once we understand this, we can celebrate Mass as we should, because we know who we are and how we relate to the one to whom we are speaking. We know Jesus himself is speaking *with us, in us*, and *through us*. Because we have *become Christ*, we dare to declare at the beginning of Mass that we are celebrating "*in the name* of the Father, and of the Son, and of the Holy Spirit." And it is with this awareness that we live with our families, work at our jobs, and recreate with our friends. We have *become Christ*. In everything we do, we are aware of "*Christ in us*, the hope of glory!" (see Colossians 1:27).

Every time we see anyone whom we can presume to be living by God's divine life, we should think, "*Christ in you*, the hope of glory!" It would be even better, when circumstances allow, to say it aloud as a greeting.

Christ in Us

Paul said these three words summed up everything he was sent by God to preach: "*Christ in you*." And he added, "the hope of glory" (Colossians 1:27). How is that for a short summary of Christianity?

Is that what we are most conscious of when we think about what it means to be a Christian? Do we get up every morning to let Christ live and act in us? Is this the glory we find in every moment of our life? Is it what makes our lives matter? Does it, for us, make others' lives matter?

When we ask what it means to be a Christian, the first thing that should overwhelm us with joy is the realization that we share in the divine life of God. And it is filled with promise. It is our assured "hope of glory." We will enjoy it forever.

Jesus tells us to make this awareness of our identity the starting point of our Christian life. "When you pray, say: 'Father'..." (Luke 11:2).

Let's get down to earth. I happen to be writing this from the Poor Clare monastery in Huehuetenango, Guatemala. Outside my window a workman named Neri Hernandez Martinez is passing by, pushing a wheelbarrow full of dirt from a drainage ditch he is digging. So we just played our little game. I called out to him through the window, "*Cristo en Neri, la esperanza de la gloria*!" Laughing, Neri turned toward me, dropped to his knees, and made the sign of the cross. Then he got up, still laughing, and continued pushing his wheelbarrow.

We both just had a "mystical experience," a moment of being consciously aware of the presence and action of God. The truth, the real truth, is that Jesus Christ just passed by, pushing a wheelbarrow in Neri, his body on earth. And if I were to go out and put a marker on the ditch he is digging that reads, "This ditch was dug by Jesus Christ," it would be nothing but the truth. The gospel truth (see Matthew 25:40, 45).

My practical suggestion—and don't laugh at it until you try it—is to use Paul's words frequently as a greeting to those with whom your relationship allows it: "*Christ in you, the hope of glory*!" I have been surprised at how easily I can say this to many people, and how well they receive it.

If we say it often enough, we won't see anyone in the same way anymore. Or ourselves either. If we keep saying to God, "*Our Father, who art in heaven*," we will soon be saying to everyone we deal with, "*Christ in you, the hope of glory.*"

Then we will understand what it means to be Christian.

How Did Jesus Relate to the Father?

"The Father loves the Son...and shows him all that he himself is doing."
JOHN 3:35; 5:20; 10:17

Only one time, in all four gospels, does Jesus speak specifically of the Father as one who punishes. It is in a parable about a king who canceled the debt of a servant who owed him thousands of dollars. Then the king learned that the same man had a fellow servant jailed who owed him only ten dollars. In anger, the king said, "Shouldn't you have had mercy on your fellow servant, as I did on you?" And he "handed him over to the jailers until he could pay his entire debt." Jesus concluded, "So my heavenly Father will also do to every one of you, if you do not forgive your brother or sister from your heart" (see Matthew 18:23ff.).

The parable is not meant to be a literal description of what the Father will do. Jesus is just making the point that the Father is a forgiving God—not a punisher but a God of mercy and compassion. Jesus is saying to us, "Forgive each other's offenses" (see Matthew 6:15). Nevertheless, some of us did grow up with more fear than love for the Father. The best way to correct that is to let Jesus himself tell us what the Father is like. How, when he was on earth, did Jesus relate to the Father?

For Jesus, the Father was not a judge or punisher but the one he turned to in all his needs, the one—perhaps the only one—who understood him. The Father was his support and protector. Yes, even when his Father let him be crucified. Jesus' dying words were, "Father, into your hands I commend my spirit" (Luke 23:46).

We don't have to be stuck in feelings, images, or experiences from the past. Jesus says, "See, I am making all things new" (Revelation 21:5). We need to look at Jesus now and let him give us a new, fresh look at the Father.

We should let Jesus tell us how God feels about us. If we devote ourselves to reading the gospels, we will experience what Jesus promised: "No one knows the Father except the Son and anyone to whom the Son chooses to reveal him" (Matthew 11:27). If at Mass we open our minds to "the grace of our Lord Jesus Christ and the love of God the Father," we will experience the "communion of the Holy Spirit" that identifies the children of God.

And we will pray with understanding, *Our Father, who art in heaven.*

What Did Jesus Say about the Father?

"No one knows the Father except the Son and anyone to whom the Son chooses to reveal him." MATTHEW 11:27

Fathers love, protect, and provide. We have Jesus' own word that the Father loves and cares for us. "The Father himself loves you, because you have loved me and have believed that I came from God" (John 16:27).

And protects us: "Do not fear those who kill the body but cannot kill the soul. Are not two sparrows sold for a penny? Yet not one of them will fall to the ground apart from your Father" (Matthew 10:28–31; John 14:1–3).

And provides: "Therefore I tell you, do not worry about your life, what you will eat, or about your body, what you will wear. Consider the ravens: they neither sow nor reap, they have neither storehouse nor barn, and yet God feeds them" (Luke 12:22–24).

And provides generously: "Ask, and it will be given you; search, and you will find; knock, and the door will be opened for you. For everyone who asks receives, and everyone who searches finds, and for everyone who knocks, the door will be opened!" (Matthew 7:7–8).

We need to see the Father always the way Jesus describes him. Try saying the Our Father while washing your hands. You may find you feel uncomfortable addressing "the Father Almighty, Creator of heaven and earth," while washing your hands in the bathroom. If so, you are reducing God to God instead of letting God be your Father. Don't millions of fathers show their little children how to wash their hands and help them do it? You may be relating to God the Father as one adult to another, forgetting what Romano Guardini said: "In the eyes of God we are all in the third grade!"

So we should see God as a loving, nurturing Father helping us in the smallest details of our life. If we let the Father wash our hands with us, we will feel God's love. We will say, "*Hallowed be your name* for being close, for being involved in my everyday actions." Saying, "*Your Kingdom come!*" will remind us that while establishing global peace and justice our Father also wants to enhance everything in our private lives. "*Your will be done*" says our Father is concerned about every hair on our heads. Our Father is the God who "walks among the pots and pans" (St. Teresa of Avila, *Book of Foundations* 5.8). We can pray to our Father everywhere. For everything. Jesus did.

Every time we pray, "*Our Father, who art in heaven*," we can keep absorbing more deeply what it means to have the Father of Jesus as our Father. Every day it will come to mean more and more to us. One day, what it means to us will be our joy forever.

As it has been the joy of Jesus from all eternity.

Our Father

"Pray then in this way: Our Father..." MATTHEW 6:9

By teaching us to say *"Our"* before *"Father,"* Jesus tells us that relationship with other human beings is an inseparable element of our relationship with God. There is no purely one-on-one spirituality in Christianity, no exclusively private relationship with God, no exclusively private beatitude in heaven (see *Evangelii Gaudium* §88, 113, 178).

This makes us ask the question: Do others' lives matter to us? How much do they matter? And why? Do the lives of people with whom we are at war matter? The lives of the terminally ill? Of babies in the womb? Of those on death row? The lives of migrants who cannot survive in their own countries? Do our own lives matter, even to us? Close to 800,000 people die every year by suicide. Do their lives matter? To them? Why should they?

The answer is that, like Jesus, we "live because of the Father" (John 6:57). Our human fathers gave us life through a single act of generation. But God keeps giving us life through an ongoing act of constant creation. If God were not at this moment continuing to will each one of us into existence, we would simply fall back into nothingness. God cannot just say to any creature, "Be!" and it is. God has to hold the note. For any one of us to keep existing, God has to keep saying, *"Beeeee...."*

The fact God keeps saying it means God wants us to be. God thinks we are worth it. And because God is Love, God wants us to "be and become everything we can be" (*esse et bene esse*, St. Augustine's definition of love). Jesus said, "I came that they may have life, and have it abundantly" (John 10:10). The fullness of life is divine life. So God is giving us existence, not just to live as human beings but to live the divine life of God on earth. To live on the level of God.

Because Christians believe God calls everyone to be God's children, our attitude toward other people on earth is different from everyone else's. Differences of race, nationality, sex, and social standing make little difference to us. Our overwhelming awareness is that we are all children of God. There is no longer American or foreigner, native born or immigrant, black or white, "upper class" or "lower class"; there is no longer male or female. Now all who were "baptized into Christ"—either through sacramental baptism or "baptism of desire" (see the *Catechism of the Catholic Church*, 1260, 1281)—are "one in Christ Jesus" (see Galatians 3:26–29).

This belief is not always reflected in our behavior. That is why we need to reflect on it in our prayer. And we need to look for ways to keep ourselves conscious of it all day long—conscious both of who we are and of who others are. Conscious of their mystery and ours.

Every time we say, *"Our Father,"* it reminds us that we are all one family, brothers and sisters to one another, daughters and sons of one Father. Christianity is inclusive of all who are divine. Saying "Our Father" makes our religion a shared experience of the divine *Being, Truth, Goodness,* and *Oneness* that characterize reborn human life on earth. Our religion is an ongoing experience of mystical relationship.

"Who art in heaven..."

Our citizenship is in heaven. PHILIPPIANS 3:20

"Our citizenship is in heaven." These words change everything. Our Father is "in heaven." Our Father is not just of this world. Our Father exists on another, transcendent plane of being. And so do we. Wherever our Father lives, we have a home. The words "who art in heaven" tell us our true home is not limited to this earth. Our "citizenship is in heaven." Jesus himself said:

> Do not let your hearts be troubled....In my Father's house there are many dwelling places....I have told you that I go to prepare a place for you. And...I will come again and will take you to myself, so that where I am, there you may be also. JOHN 14:1–3

On earth we are acutely conscious that our bodies exist only in time and space, and we will soon be removed from both. "For here we have no lasting city" (Hebrews 13:14). With Isaiah (38:12) we say, "My dwelling is plucked...from me like a shepherd's tent." But the gift of divine, eternal life has changed all that. Now we say with Paul, "If the earthly tent we live in is destroyed, we have a home with God... eternal in the heavens" (2 Corinthians 5:1). We "are looking for the city that is to come." We already possess "something better and more lasting" (Hebrews 13:14; 10:34). Our Father is in heaven. And where the Father is, there is our home.

That is the mystery of our being. Because we were baptized into Christ, Son of the Father, we are not just occupants of time and space, members of the human race just "passing through." We are members of God's family. God's home is our home.

This frees us from a lot of concerns. Because "[o]ur citizenship is in heaven," St. Paul advises:

> From now on, let...those who deal with the world be as though they had no dealings with it. For the present form of this world is passing away. I want you to be free from anxieties. 1 CORINTHIANS 7:29–32

We possess eternal life. Already. It is in us. So we can afford to deal with this world—and let the world deal with us—unconcerned about anything that won't matter once we get home. Our answer to the fear of death is "*Our Father, who art in heaven....*"

> Who will separate us from the love of Christ? Will hardship, or distress, or persecution, or famine, or nakedness, or peril, or sword?...No, in all these things we are more than conquerors through him who loved us. For I am convinced that neither death, nor life, nor angels, nor rulers, nor things present, nor things to come, nor powers, nor height, nor depth, nor anything else in all creation, will be able to separate us from the love of God in Christ Jesus our Lord. ROMANS 8:35–39

This is the joy of being Christian.

Out of This World

"Let your light shine before others, so that they may see your good works and give glory to your Father in heaven." MATTHEW 5:16

God told us that, human nature being what it is, there is a limit on how good we can be. We can't be as holy as God, our *Father in heaven.*

> "For my thoughts are not your thoughts, nor are your ways my ways," says the LORD. "For as the heavens are higher than the earth, so are my ways higher than your ways and my thoughts than your thoughts." ISAIAH 55:8–9

But God changed this by promising: "A new heart I will give you, and a new spirit....I will put my Spirit within you...and you shall be my people, and I will be your God" (Ezekiel 36:26).

Jesus fulfilled this promise when he gave us "grace," the gift of sharing in the divine life of God. He brought us into "the communion of the Holy Spirit," that is, into the fellowship, *koinonia*, of those who "live by the Spirit" and are "guided by the Spirit" as divine children of God (Acts 2:38; 10:45; 2 Corinthians 13:14; Galatians 5:22).

This gives us a *new standard of morality*. No longer is being "a good human being" the highest we can aim at or hope for. Now Jesus says, "Be perfect as your heavenly Father is perfect" (Matthew 5:48). St. Paul urges us: "Do not be conformed to this world, but be *transformed* by the renewing of your minds, so that you may discern what is the will of God—first, what is *good*; second, what is *pleasing* or *acceptable* to God. And finally, what is *perfect*" (see Romans 12).

Now we can reach for the stars. We no longer have to just stay on course by keeping within the channel markers of the Law, the Ten Commandments. Now we are out on the broad, open sea, navigating by the "fixed star" that is Jesus himself. Our course is a straight line to Jesus.

Our Law is the New Law of Christ, which is summarized, though not complete, in the Sermon on the Mount (Matthew, chapters 5 to 7). This New Law is not made up of laws but of goals to aim at. The New Law points us in a direction, inspires us to "dream the impossible dream," calls us to embrace the ideals of our *Father in heaven*, to try to live as if we ourselves were God—which, as we have seen, we can actually say we are, since we share in God's own unique divine life.

God's life cannot be reduced to rules and regulations. "The Spirit breathes" with divine desires and we hear the Spirit's voice. But we do not know where those desires come from, or where they lead. "So it is with everyone who is born of the Spirit" (John 3:8). God's life is infinite *Being*, infinite *Truth* and *Goodness*, lived in a way that is indivisibly *One*. The New Law of Jesus is all contained in one simple commandment, the "new commandment," which is not a commandment at all but an impossible ideal that should inspire and guide every choice we make: "I give you a new commandment...that you love one another as I have loved you" (John 13:34; 15:12).

To love—or even try to love—like that is to live in a way that is "out of this world."

New Beginning, New End

So if anyone is in Christ, there is a new creation. Everything old has passed away; see, everything has become new!

2 CORINTHIANS 5:17

Having God for our Father gives us a new destiny, a new goal for our life. Now our constant question, whatever we are doing, should be, "How does this contribute to eternal life?"

As human children of Adam and Eve, we were created to *know*, *love*, and *serve* God the Creator by using our human natures, especially intellect and will. For this, God gave us the "natural law," which even those ignorant of God's revealed words are bound to observe:

> For what can be known about God is plain to them, because God has shown it to them. Ever since the creation of the world God's eternal power and divine nature, invisible though they are, have been understood and seen through the things God has made. So they are without excuse; for though they knew God, they did not honor God as God or give thanks to God, but they became futile in their think-

ing, and their senseless minds were darkened. Claiming to be wise, they became fools...because they exchanged the truth about God for a lie and worshiped and served the creature rather than the Creator. ROMANS 1:19–25

Then, through God's Chosen People, God gave us the Ten Commandments, clear rules for living a good human life (Deuteronomy 5:6–21). We must not murder, steal, lie, or commit adultery, for these make peaceful life in society impossible. We must respect parents and elders, because these are, or should be, our models of developed human nature. And we must adore only one God, the infinite (therefore unique) *Being*, *Truth*, *Goodness*, and *Unity* of God, without whom all values would ultimately be relative, passing, and arbitrary.

The rabbis say the Sabbath law to abstain from work once a week was to teach us that humans are unique in creation. Everything else on the planet exists only to contribute to the overall functioning of the universe. Not so humans. We were made for direct, personal relationship with God. Our work is important, even necessary, but it is not our reason for existing, our *raison d'être*. And to keep us aware of this—of what it means to be human—God commanded us to abstain from all but essential work once a week whether we feel like it or not.

We were *created* to know, love, and serve God as only human beings can. The Commandments teach us to do that. But by baptism we have been *re-created* to know and love God as God actually is: as Father, Son, and Spirit. We are called, as divine children of the Father, to live a divine life, to act on the level of God as worthy "children of the Father." Now we can see and love each other as the brothers and sisters "in Christ" that we really are, true children of the same Father. Jesus gives us a hint of what this is in his New Law.

This is beyond what created human nature is capable of. We can do it only because we have been re-created as divine. That is why we celebrate the Sabbath now on the first day of the week, the day Jesus rose from the dead and we rose "in him" to live his divine life as his divine-human body on earth. Our religion is our life: "For to us, living is Christ" (see Philippians 1:21).

Part Two

COMMITMENT TO DISCIPLESHIP

Hallowed be your name

Take a Walk

O LORD, how glorious is your name in all the earth! PSALM 8:1

Take a walk. Just look at what is in front of you: Feel wonder and joy to find the earth covered with a carpet of green grass! Feel amazement at the majesty and grandeur of trees surging from the ground. Feel delight in the contemplation of so many kinds of birds, of every differently designed and intricately colored flower. Your heart will be saying, before you speak a word, *"Hallowed be your name*!" Appreciation calls for praise.

> Praise the LORD...fire and hail, snow and frost...
> Mountains and all hills, fruit trees and all cedars!
> Wild animals and all cattle, creeping things
>   and flying birds!

Young men and women alike, old and young
   together!
Let them praise the name of the LORD,
   for God's name alone is exalted;
God's glory is above earth and heaven. PSALM 48

"Hallowed be your name!"

To enter into the mystery of Christianity, stop taking the world for granted. Imagine how sparse and bare this world could be and let yourself be filled with awe and admiration for what it actually is. In response to what you see, say, *"Hallowed be your name!"* Say it all day, every day. Live in wonderland. See magic. See mystery.

Take a walk. Ride or drive in the mountains. Swim in a lake or in the ocean. Look up at the sky, day or night. See if you don't keep exclaiming, *"Hallowed be your name!"*

Yes, there are sad things in the world, ugly things. But none of them is willed—even though permitted—by our Father. And if you have to think about the negative, keep thinking until you see how, through the death and resurrection of Jesus, continued in the countless daily deaths and resurrections of the members of his body on earth, the Father is bringing all things to a happy ending. *"Hallowed be your name!"*

The prayer Jesus taught us to say is a prayer of joy. First it awakens our faith: *"hallowed be your name!"* Then our hope: *"your kingdom come!"* Then our love in the total surrender of *"your will be done on earth as it is in heaven!"*

This is how Jesus taught us to pray: *"Hallowed be your name!"* It echoes his response to what he sees in the Father and sees expressed in the work of God's hands.

Pray the Our Father. Every morning. All day long—for example, whenever you feel anxiety or special gratitude for something. Absorb it. Let it sink in, become your ongoing, personal profession of faith, hope, and love. Say it until you see it, feel it, and embrace it as the sum of all your desires. Then wait for the day when these words will be your cry of ecstasy forever: "*Hallowed be your name*!"

A Logical Consequence

"I have called you friends, because I have made known to you everything that I have heard from my Father." JOHN 15:15

God can't lie. If Jesus tells us to make it our first priority that the Father's "Name" should be "hallowed"—"glorified," known, appreciated, and praised by everyone—and to pray for this, he must be inviting us to know and appreciate God ourselves. Otherwise, how could we lead others to do it? So God must be promising to make it possible. That is just logical.

This alone is enough to make us lose ourselves in wonder and gratitude for the love of God. God invites us to enter into personal relationship with the infinite God. Into friendship. Into personal, intimate friendship with God as God!

Our logical first step is to enter into personal friendship with Jesus, a friendship both human and divine. That is the easiest way to get to "know" the Father. Jesus said, "Whoever has seen me has seen the Father." Jesus is the mystery of the Father, Son, and Spirit made visible (John 14:1–11).

So Jesus promises to let us enter into personal friendship with him, to let us know his mind and heart and soul. Jesus, who is God, invites us into a relationship of deep, personal, intimate friendship with himself and "in him" with God.

Jesus said, "I do not call you servants any longer, because the servant does not know what the master is doing; but I have called you friends, because I have made known to you everything that I have heard from my Father" (John 15:15). This is Jesus speaking, God speaking. Every time we pray, *"Hallowed be your name!"* we can hear Jesus saying to us, "I invite you to be my intimate friend."

A natural reaction to this would be to echo what Simon Peter said when he first began to understand who Jesus was: "Go away from me, Lord, for I am a sinful man!" (Luke 5:8).

But God always has the final word. The Father knows how to convince us. "God proves his love for us in that while we still were sinners Christ died for us."

> For God so loved the world that he gave his only Son, so that everyone who believes in him may not perish but may have eternal life....And this is eternal life, that they may know you, the only true God, and Jesus Christ whom you have sent. JOHN 3:16; 17:3; SEE ROMANS 5:8

That is what God promises. That is what we are accepting to believe when we pray, *"Hallowed be your name!"* That is the promise of Christianity: the fullness of life experienced in intimate knowledge of God. And no matter how many sins we commit, the promise remains unchanged.

We might say, quoting Exodus 34:6 and John 1:14, Christianity is the religion of God's "steadfast love and faithfulness."

The Key to Relationship: Interaction

The Word became flesh and lived among us,
and we have seen his glory. JOHN 1:14

Relationships depend on interaction. To enter into personal relationship with Jesus Christ, we need to interact with him personally. The key to friendship is mutual *sharing* of mind and will and heart. That is the way Jesus described it: "I have called you friends, because I have *made known to you* everything I have heard from my Father" (John 15:15). Jesus shares with us everything the Father shares with him. He brings us into his own relationship with the Father.

The level of any relationship depends on how much of ourselves we are willing to reveal, to expose, to another. Acquaintances are willing to share information, perhaps even some of their opinions, with each other. But we are not really friends until we share our *feelings*, and the experiences they come from. And we are not friends of Jesus Christ until we try to enter into his feelings—his feelings about the Father, about himself and us, about other people. Until we ask, "What does Jesus feel about me?" we are not relating to him as a friend.

Jesus invited us to do this. On December 27, 1673, Jesus appeared to St. Margaret Mary Alacoque, a nun of the Visitation Convent in Paray-le-Monial, France, showed her his heart, and gave her the message that people should focus on his love. It was a frank revelation of his feelings: "See the heart that has loved people so much, and received so little in return." By calling us to have "devotion to his Sacred Heart," Jesus was calling us to understand his feelings and respond to them. He does the same thing when he teaches us to echo the first desire of his heart by praying, "*Hallowed be your name!*"

In committed friendships, like those of husband and wife, both parties are pledged to this. We take for granted that married couples talk to each other dependably and deeply and express their feelings, even passionately. All Christians have this same commitment to Jesus.

And what a gift it is! That Jesus Christ, God's own self, would invite us into intimate friendship with himself is unbelievable. But we have to believe it and devote ourselves to it, or we will not know the joy of being authentic Christians.

No one can interact with Jesus Christ on the personal level and remain the same. The more he shares with us, the more we know him, love him, and become like him. That sums up the mystery of our Christian life. In us Jesus is gradually bringing our thoughts into conformity with his thoughts, our desires into conformity with his desires, our way of acting as humans into conformity with his divine way of acting as God. Christian life is all about *growing* into the full experience of "this mystery, which is *Christ in us, the hope of glory*" (Colossians 1:27).

What does this mean in terms of the concrete actions we have to take in order to experience personal friendship with Jesus? We have to ask *when*, *where*, and *how* we can (and will) interact with Jesus. How will we interact with God in a way that is personal, intimate, even passionate?

The decisions we make will tell us what kind of relationship we choose to have with God.

Getting in Touch with Our Feelings

"It is out of the abundance of the heart that the mouth speaks."
LUKE 6:45

To experience—and grow more deeply into—the gift, the mystery, of personal relationship with Jesus, the logical way to begin is by reading and reflecting on his words in Scripture. But the danger is that this might be too heady, too exclusively focused on what Jesus meant rather than on what he felt. That would be to relate to him more as teacher than as friend.

When Paul writes, "Let the same mind be in you that was in Christ Jesus" (Philippians 2:5), the word "mind" does not mean just intellect. Paul is talking about the all-embracing orientation of our whole being: mind, heart, and soul. God's commandment is, "You shall love the Lord your God with all your heart, with all your soul, with all your mind" (Matthew 22:37). And Mary is the great example of this. Luke presents it as typical of her that she "treasured all these words, all these things, and pondered them in her heart" (see Luke 2:19, 51). So, when we read the words of Jesus, we need to be looking for union of heart as well as of mind. How do we do this?

The key word is "feeling." We need to ask what Jesus was feeling when he said these words, and—just as important—what we were feeling when we read them. Union of heart is not just a matter of feelings or emotions, but it can hardly be fully human without them. This is the whole point and purpose—and pain—of those moments of "dark night of the soul," to which God subjects the more advanced: all human feeling is taken out of their relationship with God so they will know unambiguously it is divine. But that need not concern us here.

For union of heart, we need to be in touch both with Jesus' feelings and with our own. When we read in the gospels what he said and did, and how people responded and failed to respond to him, we need to ask ourselves, "How did Jesus feel then? How does it make me feel?"

Jesus expressed his feelings: *joyfully*, when he (undoubtedly) danced at the wedding feast of Cana; *tenderly*, when little children came to him; *gratefully*, when Mary washed his feet (after his host hadn't); *viciously*, when he raged against some Pharisees for their hypocrisy; *angrily*, when they refused to answer him; *tearfully*, when his friend Lazarus died; *with more tears*, when Jerusalem rejected him; *happily*, when Peter acknowledged him as Messiah; *sorrowfully*, when he told his apostles one would betray him and all the rest abandon him; *reproachfully*, when his disciples failed to support him during his agony in the garden; *nakedly*, when he felt on the cross that the Father had abandoned him; *triumphantly* to his disciples after rising from the dead.

If we share Christ's feelings—for example, his zeal, his passion to glorify the Father, his enthusiasm to establish the Kingdom on earth—it is some evidence we are in union of heart as well as mind with Jesus. And that helps us achieve the goal we are aiming at here, which is to recognize and rejoice in the mystery that we are invited into felt, experienced union with God in mind and will and heart. We realize we can "know you, the only true God, and Jesus Christ whom you have sent" (John 17:3). And we want to. That is what we are saying when we pray, "*Hallowed be your name!*"

How to Use Our Feelings

"Not everyone who says to me, 'Lord, Lord,' will enter the kingdom of heaven, but only the one who does the will of my Father in heaven."
MATTHEW 7:21

Feelings are not free choices. We have little or no control over how we feel, although we might have control, sometimes, over the causes that produce our feelings. In themselves, emotions are neither good nor bad. We are never better or worse because of anything we feel, desire, want to do, or don't want to do. Nothing makes us good or bad except our free choices.

However, feelings can be good sources of information, if we know how to read them. Feelings can tell us a lot about our deep attitudes and values, which are often rooted in free acts of intellect and will. Feelings can even be a clue to what God is saying to us. If we know the difference between sentiment and stance, feeling union with Jesus can sometimes assure us our relationship with him is personal and real. So our feelings, although they are never to be taken at face value, are something we should take seriously. How, then, do we deal with feelings?

First, we have to recognize them. A form of prayer St. Ignatius recommended highly is the "Consciousness Examen" (*Spiritual Exercises*, nos. 24–43) or "Awareness Exercise." In it, the first step is to look at our feelings and how they may have changed during the day.

To get in touch with our feelings, we ask, "Was I in a good mood or a bad mood when I got up? Did that change as the day went on? When? Do I now feel encouraged or discouraged? Enthusiastic, half-hearted, or turned off? Peaceful or disturbed? About what?"

The next step is to ask *why*, to look for the cause of these feelings. "When did my mood change? Was it because of something I saw, heard, or thought? Something someone did to me, or something

I did? Did my mood change—for better or worse—because of something I decided to do?"

The third step is to discern. "Could it be that my mood changed, not just because of natural causes, but because God is saying something to me, telling me something by turning on or off the good feelings I have about my relationship with God, about the ideals, goals, and work I have accepted? Is Jesus showing me I am in touch or out of touch with his heart?"

When God is behind them, the technical names for these mood changes are "consolation" and "desolation" (*Spiritual Exercises*, 316–17, 322). But for our purpose, let's just call them the presence or absence of felt union of heart with Jesus. When, with our will, we *want* to be completely one with Jesus, but we don't *feel* it, we need to ask some questions. Have our feelings changed because God is telling us we are no longer "on the beam" but have strayed off course because of some decision we have made? If so, we had better reconsider that decision. If not, we just accept the absence of feeling as God's way of showing us we are not in control.

Sometimes our deepest experience of union with Jesus is just missing the feeling when it is absent.

How We Know God

"The Holy Spirit...will teach you everything, and remind you of all that I have said to you." JOHN 14:26

When we pray *"Hallowed be your name!"* we are wanting the Father to be known and loved by everyone, beginning with ourselves, the way the Father is known and loved by Jesus himself.

But that is clearly impossible. Jesus himself said so: "No one knows the Son except the Father, and no one knows the Father except the Son"; then he went on to say, "and anyone to whom the Son chooses to reveal him" (see Matthew 11:27). But Jesus can't reveal the Father to us! No human being can possibly know the Father—not as the Father really is. God is "infinite," without limits, without boundaries. But humans understand things in clearly limited "thoughts." And every thought is like a photograph, a "still shot." It just shows us one tiny part of reality.

Knowing God is knowing *all* of reality at once. We can't get God into one thought. And even if we could, to really understand the Father as Father we would have to *be* the Son. Jesus is the *only* Son of the Father, God the Son, second Person of the Holy Trinity. The relationship between the Father and the Son is unique. No created nature can possibly experience it.

So the only possible way Jesus can let us know the Father as he does is by joining us to himself, sharing with us his own divine life as God the Son. Specifically, he must let us share in his own, personal, divine act of knowing the Father. Jesus alone knows God as "Father." And it is only by knowing *in him*, "in Christ," as members of his body, that we can know the Father as Father.

This is the second great mystery and joy of Christianity. By the "grace of the Lord Jesus Christ," the favor of sharing in Christ's own divine life, we can *know* God the Father as the Son does. This is friendship with God. We are called into the intimacy of personal relationship with God.

What do we have to do to get there? It is very simple. Given grace, we become friends with Jesus the same way we become friends with anyone else. And how is that?

First, we have to spend some *time* with Jesus. If we don't choose to do that, we don't choose to be friends with him. People who won't take time to date never get married. Married couples who don't take time to be with each other have a bad or mediocre marriage. It's a simple, either-or choice. But if people will take time to really get to know each other—and to keep knowing each other more and more deeply—the payoff is fantastic. And the same is true with Jesus.

Growing in knowledge and appreciation of Jesus is the most exciting thing in life. Jesus said so: "I came that they may have life, and have it abundantly....And this is eternal life, that they may *know you*, the only true God, and Jesus Christ whom you have sent" (John 10:10; 17:3). Try it and see. Give a few minutes a day to the three Rs. You will find your *reading*, *reflecting*, and *responding* transfigured into *remembering*, *realizing*, and *rejoicing*.

And you will find that your religion is the greatest joy of your life.

Developing Friendship with God

"Lord, to whom can we go? You have the words of eternal life."
JOHN 6:68

So we set aside some time to spend with Jesus. What do we do with the time?

The answer is, the same thing we do when we spend good time, personal time, with anybody—we share. We ask personal questions and reveal personal things about ourselves. We listen a lot and try to absorb what we hear. So if we want to know what Jesus thinks and how he feels about things, we let him tell us. We read his words in Scripture and think about what they mean—that is, about what they meant to him when he said them and what he wants them to mean to us now.

And we argue with him, knowing he is right but asking why. To argue is to take another's opinion seriously, to confront it. We think about what Jesus says, ask what we agree or don't agree with, trying to come to agreement. We fit what he says into the context of his life, asking how he lived it out and what difference it will make in ours if we try to put it into practice.

With Jesus, instead of asking what we *should* do, it is sometimes more practical to ask what we could do or would do. Jesus is always asking us for more than we are able, or willing, to give. That is what makes him so exciting. He never lets us stagnate. But all he really insists on is forward motion. The devil's strategy is to discourage us. Jesus just asks us to do what we can now, and he will help us do more tomorrow. Isn't that what friends do?

When Jesus invited people to "follow" him (e.g., Matthew 4:19; 9:9), it was so they could listen to more of what he had to say. So if we truly want to be disciples (the word means "students") of the mind and heart of Jesus, we have to "sign up" and commit ourselves to studying his words on a regular basis. What this comes down to in practice is committing ourselves to the three Rs of discipleship: to *read*, *reflect*, and *respond*.

But for our commitment to mean anything, we have to get down to the nitty gritty. Humans act in space and time. *When* will I read Scripture? *Where*? For *how long*? And *what* Bible will I use? Do I have a copy? Until I can picture myself in a particular place and at a specific time, doing what I propose, I haven't made a human commitment.

We enter into personal relationship with Jesus by filling our minds with knowledge of his mind, bringing our hearts into union with his heart. This was, and still is, St. Paul's prayer for us:

> I pray that you may have the power to comprehend, with all the saints, what is the breadth and length and height and depth, and to know the love of Christ that surpasses knowledge, so that you may be filled with all the fullness of God. EPHESIANS 3:18–19

So it is our gift and glory as Christians to enter into *personal relationship with God*. But before this becomes part of our being, it has to become part of our daily routine. We are pledging ourselves to this when we pray, "*Hallowed be your name!*" We become disciples when we do it.

"*I Will Return...*"

So he set off and went to his father. But while he was still far off, his father saw him and was filled with compassion; he ran and put his arms around him and kissed him. LUKE 15:20

The prodigal son story is really about a father, one whose son wanted only what his father could give him—first his inheritance; then, after he squandered that, food and shelter. He didn't know, and didn't really love, his father.

To be forgiven, the son thought he had to confess his sin. "I will go to my father, and say, 'Father, I have sinned.'" But the father never let him finish. He "threw his arms around him, kissed him," and called for the fatted calf. The Church teaches that God does the same with us. Forgiveness doesn't depend on "going to confession." Our Father loves us more than that.

The *Catechism of the Catholic Church*, no. 1457, says we have to confess our "mortal" sins to a priest "unless...." The "unless" makes it perfectly clear that the Church believes God forgives sins without confession; otherwise, there could be no "unless."

The *Catechism* also makes it clear that Mother Church's law does not require confession before Communion, even for mortal sins, if, first, we have a "grave reason" for receiving Communion, and, second, there is "no possibility" of going to confession. If these two conditions exist when we are at Mass, it is enough to ask pardon from our Father in our heart, with the intention of going to confession when possible. Then we should go ahead and eat at our Father's table. Our Mother, the Church, says we should never miss Communion for lack of confession.

Obviously, the most "serious reason" there is for receiving Communion is the simple fact that it is the Body and Blood of Jesus Christ, and Jesus said, "Unless you eat the flesh of the Son of Man and drink his blood, you have no life in you" (John 6:53). So this first condition always exists. And, given the importance of Communion as proclaimed by Jesus, wouldn't it be a very "grave" sin (I don't say "mortal") to deprive anyone of Communion who has the right to receive?

The second condition is that there is "no possibility" of confession because no priest is available. In the mind of the Church, always a loving Mother, "no possibility" is not absolute. For example, if a woman guilty of adultery is at Mass, longing for reconciliation and Communion, and there is a priest right there, sitting in the confessional, would any bishop in the Catholic Church say it is "possible" for her to go to confession to him if he happens to be her own son? She should ask pardon from God, receive Communion, and confess her sin when another priest is available.

Wouldn't the same reasoning apply when one does not want to confess to a particular priest, not because of any difficulty inherent in confession as such (normally, relief should overcome reluctance), but because one has a special reason for not feeling confidence in this priest? Then, for practical purposes, there is "no priest available," and the law allows one to receive Communion and put off confession until a priest is available with whom the sacrament can be what it should be: a joyful deliverance with encouraging guidance to continuing conversion.

If we are sorry for our sins, we should *never* miss Communion for lack of confession. We should receive Jesus with gratitude to our Father and say, *"Hallowed be your name!"*

What Does God Call "Mortal" Sin?

Confess your sins to one another, and pray for one another, so that you may be healed. JAMES 5:16

If we understand clearly what we are obliged to confess, and what we are not, we can appreciate the sacrament of reconciliation not as something we *have* to do but as something we *get* to do.

We are only "obliged" to confess to a priest a sin that is truly "mortal"—that is, by theological definition, an act so *evil* that a person who did it would deserve to be burned in the fires of hell (however we understand the imagery) for all eternity. If we don't believe that some act denounced from the pulpit as "mortal sin" is so evil that a loving Christian mother would agree her daughter should be burned at the stake for doing it, how can we say we believe our infinitely loving Father would do it to any one of God's own sons or daughters? We should be very reluctant to declare positively that any particular act is sufficiently "grave matter" to be a "mortal" sin." That would be making a judgment about our Father. It might be blasphemy.

The logic is inescapable. Either we say a particular act deserves to be punished in the fires of hell for all eternity or we don't call that act a mortal sin. That is simply Catholic doctrine. So when we prepare to confess our sins, instead of "examining our conscience" for "mortal" sins (often nonexistent) that will separate us from God for all eternity, we will "examine our consciousness" instead, looking for opinions, value judgments, habitual ways of speaking and acting that

A FRESH LOOK AT THE OUR FATHER

diminish our union of mind and will and heart with God and with others. The sacrament of reconciliation then becomes for us an explicit, deliberate effort to "Let the same mind be in us that was in Christ Jesus" (Philippians 2:5). Our focus will not be on rules but on relationships: on how we have been living out the relationship we have with the Father, Son, and Spirit and with every human on earth. Our examination of conscience will be like discussing honestly and lovingly with a spouse or close friend the good and bad moments of our relationship. It should draw us closer together in mutual understanding, acceptance, and trust.

Then the act of "confessing," of putting into words, whatever we recognize and regret as imperfect will itself be an eloquent expression of love. Love not expressed is dormant. Love expressed, like the "quality of mercy," is twice blessed: it blesses the one who speaks and the one who hears. It draws them together in a shared, experienced union of mind and will and heart. That is the special value of confessing our sins—as well as our difficulties and desires—to one another or, where privacy is an issue, to a priest in the secrecy of the confessional.

Socrates said, "The unexamined life is not worth living." But we Christians have a sacrament of the examined life. Confession is something built into our lifestyle that invites us to examine our lives periodically and, in so doing, to bring our minds and hearts into growing conformity with the mind and heart of God. Every confession should move us to say with greater understanding and conviction, *"Hallowed be your name!"*

And every confession should make us appreciate our religion more for keeping us in growthful interaction with God.

A Serious Talk with Jesus

Jesus perceived...that they were discussing these questions among themselves; and he said to them, "Why do you raise such questions in your hearts?" MARK 2:8

Every Christian needs to have this dialogue with Jesus:

Lord, you really want me to pray, "*Hallowed be your name*," yes?

Yes.

And you want me to make it my first priority in life that the Father should be known and appreciated by everyone, not just superficially, but, as far as possible, as God deserves?

Yes.

And I can't possibly do this unless I know God in a deep, personal way myself?

Yes.

And you say that the best way for me to know the Father is to know you as you revealed and are still revealing yourself in your human nature?

Yes.

So am I right in saying you are promising me that if I pray, "*Hallowed be your name!*" and try to get to know you by reading and reflecting over your words and actions in the gospels, and try to respond to them appropriately in action as best I can, you will make me your personal friend?

Yes.

And you promise that now, while I am still alive on earth, you and I will have a real, personal friendship, one that is like, but better than, the relationships I have with my best friends?

Yes.

And I don't have to be "perfect," or like a saint, for this. I just have to try to get to know and love you?

Yes. But, as in every friendship, "the measure you give will be the measure you get back" (see Luke 6:38).

And this will make me happy?

Yes. Beyond anything you can imagine.

So I would be a fool not to take you up on this?

Yes.

And if I don't, it would be inconsistent with what I am asking for when I pray, "*Hallowed be your name!*"

Yes.

So do I really have a choice?

You always have a choice. Why don't you make it now?

Part Three

DEDICATION TO MISSION

"Your Kingdom come"

"Proclaim the Good News"

The Lord appointed seventy [-two] others and sent them...to proclaim the good news." LUKE 10:1; MATTHEW 10:7

The first mystery, proclaimed by the words "*Our Father*," is the *divine identity* we have through our relationship with God as daughters and sons of the Father. The second, "*Hallowed be your name*," is that we can know and make known the Father's "name," his personal self, revealed to us through *discipleship*. We are invited into personal relationship as intimate friends of God.

Now, "*Your kingdom come!*" tells us we are chosen as coworkers of Jesus himself to establish the reign of God on earth. We have a special relationship with Jesus and with everyone who is working to establish the Kingdom. United by a common goal, a common responsiveness to the guiding voice of the Spirit, we are one in the "communion [*koinonia*] of the Holy Spirit."

So the third basic mystery and joy of Christianity is that we have been selected to carry on the mission of Jesus as *evangelizers*. We were dedicated to this at baptism, when we were solemnly anointed with chrism and consecrated *prophets* to bear witness to the Good News.

Our first step as *prophets* is to proclaim the Good News that, with the coming of Jesus, the reign of God has begun. God is freeing us from enslavement to the darkness of cultural values and distortions. The present state of the world is changing. Jesus has come to make "all things new" (Revelation 21:5). There is a "new teaching" (Mark 1:27), a "new wine" (Mark 2:22), a "new self" (Ephesians 4:24; Colossians 3:10), a "new creation" (2 Corinthians 5:17; Galatians 6:15), a "new humanity" (Ephesians 2:15), a "new life of the Spirit" (Romans 7:6), a "new covenant" (Luke 22:20; 2 Corinthians 3:6; Hebrews 8:8, 9:15, 12:24). The power of sin, though not abolished, is broken. In Christ "a new age has dawned, the long reign of sin is ended, a broken world is being renewed, and humanity is once again made whole" (Easter Preface IV).

We are children of the Light. But we can only proclaim this news credibly through the *witness* of a lifestyle that raises "irresistible questions" that cannot be answered without it (Paul VI, *Evangelization in the Modern World* 21). Our lifestyle must be a way of living not determined by cultural conformity or static laws but by constant response to the Holy Spirit in living the divine Life of God. This implies a commitment to *continual conversion* and change.

Before ascending into heaven, Jesus gave us the Great Commission:

> All authority in heaven and on earth has been given to me. Go therefore and make disciples of all nations, baptizing them in the name of the Father and of the Son and of the Holy Spirit, and teaching them to obey everything I have commanded you. And remember, I am with you always, to the end of the age. MATTHEW 28:18–23

We get up in the morning with that commission and empowerment ringing in our ears. And lest we should forget it, we remind ourselves of it every morning by praying in the Our Father, "*Your Kingdom come!*" Then we go out to announce the Good News through the witness of a lifestyle that cannot be explained without it. This is our religion. What is more inspiring?

A Joint Enterprise

"You did not choose me but I chose you...to go and bear fruit."
JOHN 15:16

To our surprise, when we pray, "*Your Kingdom come!*" the first response of the Father is, "Make it happen!" Establishing the reign of God on earth is a joint enterprise, an endeavor that is both human and divine. We can't do it without God, and God won't do it without us.

Of course, the key player on the human side is Jesus. He did not proclaim, "The time is fulfilled, and the kingdom of God has come near" until he came to earth and began his mission. But then the first thing he did was to enlist humans to help him. Mark's next verses say:

> As Jesus passed along the Sea of Galilee, he saw Simon and his brother Andrew casting a net into the sea...and said to them, "Follow me and I will make you fish for people."... As he went a little farther, he saw James...and his brother John....Immediately he called them; and they...followed him. MARK 1:15–16FF.

The phrase "*Your Kingdom come*" tells us two things about our Father:

- First, our Father is not a remote deist god who does not get involved in human affairs. Our God is part of the action. God wants to reign over every area and activity of human life on earth. In Jesus and in us, Christ's body, the Father "is still working" (John 5:17).
- Second, humans are to be God's instruments in this. Jesus made that clear: "I chose you...to go and bear fruit....The Father will give you whatever you ask him in my name" (John 15:16).

When Jesus taught us to pray, "*Hallowed be your name*," he called us to enter into the gift of *faith* by which he lets us share in his own divine knowledge of the Father. We believe we can have a truly personal relationship with God. Now, in teaching us to pray, "*Your Kingdom come*," Jesus calls us into the gift of *hope*, giving us the certitude that he intends to use us as his instruments and coworkers to carry out his mission. Our confidence comes from knowing we have been personally selected and chosen to help establish the Kingdom, the reign of God on earth. We were officially commissioned, committed, and consecrated to this through our baptismal anointing as *prophets*.

In addition to proclaiming divine *Truth*, we bear witness to the divine *Good* that only God reveals, modeled to us by Jesus the Son, a Good that we in turn are to model to others until all are *One* in sharing the divine *Being* that is the *Life* of God.

Christianity is not just our religion. It is our mission. It transforms everything we say and do. And through us, God is transforming everything and everyone on earth.

Meaning through Mission

"Peace be with you. As the Father has sent me, so I send you." JOHN 20:21

What Jesus lived and breathed for every day, his priority in life, was that the Father should be known and loved: "*Hallowed be your name!*" This is salvation, life to the full: "that they may *know you*, the only true God, and Jesus Christ whom you have sent" (John 10:10; 17:3).

Jesus' second priority was to establish the reign of God on earth: "*Your Kingdom come!*" If we make these two priorities ours, our whole life becomes a *mission*. We wake up every morning with something to do, something to accomplish, something to live and work and die for that is more important than anything else human beings can do. It is to make God known and loved and to bring about what the Preface for the Solemnity of Christ the King announces:

> A kingdom of truth and life,
> A kingdom of holiness and grace,
> A kingdom of justice, love and peace.

This gives purpose, meaning, and value to everything we do. Everything that contributes to the reign of God on earth has eternal value for the whole human race. And anything that does not contribute to his reign has ultimately no value at all. Paul warns us against flying blind:

> Do you not know that in a race the runners all compete, but only one receives the prize? Run in such a way that you may win it. Athletes exercise self-control in all things; they do it to receive a perishable crown, but we an imperishable one. So we do not run aimlessly, nor do we box as though beating the air. 1 CORINTHIANS 9:24–26

It sounds very radical to say that anything that does not contribute to making God known and establishing his Kingdom on earth is ultimately worthless. But think about it. What use is it to do something that does not contribute in any way to "truth and life...holiness and grace...justice, love and peace"? Put "everlasting" in front of all those nouns. The epitaph on a pre-Christian Greek tombstone (echoed more positively by Job 1:21) reads:

> Naked at my birth
> Naked back to earth.
> What's it worth?
> Fool I to work and earn and spend,
> For a naked end!

To pray, "*Your Kingdom come!*" every morning gives direction, purpose, and meaning to everything we do. In our family and social life, work and civic involvement, we will be conscious of our mission to make everything contribute to the truth and goodness, unity and peace that belong to the Kingdom of God.

That is a mission, and a religion, worth waking up for!

A Practical Object of Choice

"You will receive power when the Holy Spirit has come upon you; and you will be my witnesses...to the ends of the earth." ACTS 1:8

Jesus began his mission announcing the Good News as a practical object of choice, something we can get involved in here and now. He has arrived as Messiah and begun to establish his reign over every area and activity of human life on earth. It is something we can start doing with him. Jesus is inviting us all to join him now as "prophets"—coworkers and "missionary disciples." Now.

> Jesus came to Galilee, proclaiming the good news of God,
> and saying, "The time is fulfilled, and the Kingdom of God
> has come near. Repent, and believe in the good news."
> MARK 1:14; MATTHEW 4:17

"Repent" doesn't just mean to turn away from sin. It is to turn *toward* everything that is good and true and beautiful in the Good News. It is *metanoia*, a complete change of mind—of attitudes, values, goals, and behavior. Isaiah (48:6) proclaims "new things, hidden things that you have not known." God is saying, "See, I am making all things new" (Revelation 21:5).

The reign of Christ is enlightenment and empowerment. Jesus said, "I tell you, the one who believes in me will also do the works that I do"—by faith and the power of the Spirit—"and, in fact, will do greater works than these, because I am going to the Father" (John 14:12).

What empowers us is surrender. When Mary said, "Let it be with me according to your word," the Word was made flesh in her. When we say the same, our surrender empowers us to live on the level of God and to let the words of Jesus be made flesh in our lifestyle. When we do that visibly, it is called "*prophetic witness.*" A radical change of lifestyle is the first step we are called to make in fulfillment of our mission to establish the Kingdom of God. It gives us credibility.

When we let the words "*Your Kingdom come!*" inspire us to bear witness by our lifestyle a little more each day, we grow into the mystery of prophetic living, living visibly as Christians in a way that cannot be explained without the Good News. Our morning prayer should launch us into this mystery and help it gradually transform our whole way of life "until we all become one in faith and in the knowledge of

God's Son, and *form that perfect human* who is *Christ come to full stature*" (Ephesians 4:13).

Our religion is mission, a mission to which our baptismal consecration as *prophets* commits us. It is the mission to which we rededicate ourselves every time we pray, "*Your Kingdom come!*"

Our religion, without dedication to mission, is unintelligible. With dedication to mission, it is unbeatable.

And it is ours for the choosing. Now.

The Kingdom Includes Everything

"All authority in heaven and on earth has been given to me."
MATTHEW 28:18

Because we believe the "Father almighty" is "one God, Creator of heaven and earth," the kingdom over which the Father reigns embraces "all things visible and invisible." Everything humans do, large or small, physical or intellectual, remarkable or hardly noticeable, has some effect, positive or negative, on the Kingdom of God. That makes everything we do "in Christ," as members of his body, divinely important, eternally important. Pope Francis urges us:

> You need to see the entirety of your life as a mission. Try to do so by listening to God in prayer and recognizing the signs he gives you. Always ask the Spirit what Jesus expects from you at every moment of your life and in every decision you must make, so as to discern its place in the mission you have received. *REJOICE AND BE GLAD* 23

Changing diapers has eternal value as the fulfillment of our mission to love. Like mercy, it blesses those who receive and those who give (see *The Merchant of Venice*), because love gives life, and those who give receive. So does washing dishes, filling out forms, answering the phone, selling insurance, repairing cars, managing a company, holding political office—if all is done with love, in love, and for love to give God's life to the world. As Francis says, we "need to see the entirety of our life as a mission." So in everything we do, we can pray, "*Your Kingdom come!*" and work to bring it about in large ways and small.

Everything counts. Jesus promised it: "I chose you. And I appointed you to go and bear fruit, fruit that will last, so that the Father will give you whatever you ask in my name" (John 15:16).

With confidence we can pray every morning to the Father in Jesus' name, "*Your Kingdom come!*" and then go out every day and work to make it real. If we pray this every day, our mission will become the abiding motivation of our lives.

And our religion will be the leaven of our lives, a force in us that makes all our interactions with this world grow in grandeur.

Humility is truth. So it is not against humility if we say that to live as a Christian is to be God's blessing to the human race.

A Lifestyle That Raises Eyebrows

"Take no gold, or silver, or copper in your belts." MATTHEW 10:9

To invite people credibly to believe the Good News, we have to make it evident that we ourselves, by accepting Christ's reign over us, have been "delivered from darkness and the shadow of death," that is, from slavery to our culture. The only way we can do that is by living an enlightened and emancipated lifestyle so different and so far beyond what is normal for humans that it would not be possible without "the grace of the Lord Jesus Christ," that is, the gift of sharing in the divine life of God—which is the Good News.

For the definition of prophetic witness, Pope Francis frequently quotes Pope Paul VI's encyclical *Evangelization in the Modern World*, no. 21:

> Above all the Gospel must be proclaimed by witness. Take a Christian or a handful of Christians who, in the midst of their own community, show their capacity for understanding and acceptance, their sharing of life and destiny with other people, their solidarity with the efforts of all for whatever is noble and good. Let us suppose that, in addition, they radiate faith in values that go beyond current values, and hope in something not seen, that one would not dare to imagine. Through this wordless witness they stir up irresistible questions in the hearts of those who see how they live: "Why are they like this? Why do they live in this way? What or who is it that inspires them? Why are they in our midst?" Such a witness is already a silent proclamation of the Good News.

Every time we pray, "*Your Kingdom come*!" our prayer invites us to live a lifestyle that raises eyebrows. Christians should not "fit in." Jesus said that would be an identifying mark of his followers: "If you belonged to the world, the world would love you as its own. Because you do not belong to the world, but I have chosen you out of the world—therefore the world hates you" (John 15:19).

That isn't as daunting as it sounds. There is a very simple way to turn our whole life into Christian witness. We just need to ask, before everything we say and do, "How does this bear witness to the values of Jesus?" We decide *never to ask again just whether something is right or wrong* but to ask instead whether it follows from, and gives expression to, something taught by Jesus.

That changes our whole standard of morality. We don't have to always *do* what bears witness; few people are that perfect, and to expect this of ourselves could be discouraging. But Jesus knows that if we just ask the question constantly, "*How does this bear witness to Christ?*" it will give us a different mind-set. And he will settle for that. Little by little, it will transform our lives.

Praying "*Your Kingdom come!*" every morning will remind us to do that.

Living by the New Law

"Do not think that I have come to abolish the law or the prophets; I have come not to abolish but to fulfill." MATTHEW 5:17

To live a life of Christian witness, it is not enough just to keep the Ten Commandments and obey all the rules. Those who did that best— most visibly, at least—in the time of Jesus were the scribes, defenders of traditional religion, and the Pharisees, strict interpreters of the law. But of them Jesus said, "I tell you, unless your righteousness exceeds that of the scribes and Pharisees, you will never enter the Kingdom of heaven" (Matthew 5:20). We must live by the New Law.

The New Law of Jesus begins where the Ten Commandments leave off. The Commandments are rules for good human behavior. The New Law gives guidelines for living on the level of God.

Just living by the Ten Commandments doesn't usually raise eyebrows. Nor does it keep us from "belonging to the world" or make the world "hate us" (John 15:19). The wisdom of the Ten Commandments is obvious to any thinking person. Moses told the Jews:

> See, just as the LORD my God has charged me, I now teach you statutes and ordinances....You must observe them diligently, for this will show your wisdom and discernment to the peoples, who, when they hear all these statutes, will say, "Surely this great nation is a wise and discerning people!"
> DEUTERONOMY 4:5–6

Christian wisdom, on the other hand, the New Law of Jesus, is unintelligible except by the divine light of faith, given by the Holy Spirit. Paul made that clear:

> We speak of these things in words not taught by human wisdom but taught by the Spirit, interpreting spiritual things to those who are spiritual. Those who are unspiritual do not receive the gifts of God's Spirit, for they are foolishness to them, and they are unable to understand them because they are spiritually discerned. 1 CORINTHIANS 2:13–14

Even baptized Christians may not be spiritual enough to accept the New Law of Jesus in the full, practical way Paul had in mind. He wrote to his converts in Corinth:

> And so, brothers and sisters, I could not speak to you as spiritual people, but rather as people of the flesh, as infants in Christ. I fed you with milk, not solid food, for you were not ready for solid food. Even now you are still not ready.
> 1 CORINTHIANS 3:1–2

Praying daily "*Your Kingdom come!*" will help make us ready by reminding us that God's Kingdom, even on earth, is beyond all human morality: "a kingdom of truth and life, holiness and grace, justice, love, and peace." It calls us to *discipleship*, to the study of God's own divine mind and will expressed in the divine-human words of Scripture. It motivates us to go beyond law observance and live lives of Christian, prophetic *witness*—"until we grow to maturity, to the measure of the full stature of Christ" (Ephesians 4:13). This is authentic Christianity. It is what we dedicate ourselves to do when we pray, "*Your Kingdom come!*"

Part Four

SURRENDER TO MINISTRY

"Your will be done on earth as it is in heaven"

An Invitation to Spousal Love

"I do not call you servants any longer, because the servant does not know what the master is doing; but I have called you friends, because I have made known to you everything that I have heard from my Father." JOHN 15:15

Here our focus changes from *what* to *who*, from what we want to do—establish the Kingdom—to the person with whom we want to be united. Now we are looking at the Person of the Father, desiring that the whole world be totally surrendered to God, beginning with ourselves.

In teaching us to pray, *"Your will be done on earth as it is in heaven,"* Jesus tells us we are not just called to carry out God's orders and achieve the Father's goals on earth. We must make the Father's will our will and already on earth be as completely united to God's own self as those in heaven are.

For this we have to be one with the Father, in total union of mind and heart as well as of will. Without this overall union, there is no way God's will can be done on earth as it is in heaven. Heaven is the state of perfect, total union with God:

> Beloved, we are God's children now; what we will be has not yet been revealed. What we do know is this: when God is revealed, we will be like God, for we will see God as God is. 1 JOHN 3:2

To do exactly and totally what another wills, we have to think like the other, feel like the other, and be of one mind and will and heart with the other. Paul asked his converts to "be of the same mind, having the same love, being in full accord and of one mind....Let the same mind be in you that was in Christ Jesus" (Philippians 2:2–5).

This is the relationship of spousal love. The specific—in fact, unique—love of the married is a mutual, lifelong pledge to keep doing whatever leads to perfect union of mind and will and heart:

- union of *mind* by *sharing*, dialoguing, trying to understand each other's views. With God we practice the three Rs of *discipleship*: reading, reflecting, and responding to God's words.
- union of *will* by being willing to *change*, trying to accept whatever principles, ideals, goals, or values in one's spouse are higher than one's own. With God this means *continual conversion*, constant changes in our way of life, seeking to bear convincing witness to the Good News.

- union of *heart* by shedding our protective armor of reserve and expressing our emotions spontaneously, until we are totally comfortable being ourselves with each other. With God we *surrender* to letting Christ express himself without reserve in our words and actions. That means giving human, physical expression to our faith, hope, and love.

When we pray, *"Your will be done on earth as it is in heaven,"* we are pledging to pursue spousal love with the infinite Person(s) of God! That is the astonishing mystery and joy of being Christian. Our religion is the expression and experience of spousal love with God.

The Mystery of Oneness

"The glory you have given to me I have given them, so that they may be one, as we are one." JOHN 17:22

The mystery of *Oneness* is almost a non-thought with us. We know God as infinite *Being*, *Truth*, and *Goodness*. We also know God as *One*, but that doesn't seem to have much to do with us. We relate to the need to be truthful and good. Those are goals we can strive for. But to *"be one,"* as the Father, Son, and Spirit are one, how do we go about doing that?

Yet infinite *Oneness* is a trait of God, as awesome as infinite *Being*, *Truth*, and *Goodness*. To appreciate that oneness, and to cultivate the integrity and wholeness of our own being, plus oneness with God and others, is essential to being an authentic Christian.

A guideline to the realization of this Oneness is a line from Paul's letter to the Galatians (4:19): "My little children, for whom I am again in the pain of childbirth until Christ is formed in you." We are not formed Christians until "Christ is formed" in us. To be "perfect" is not a matter of working against constant, recurring temptations and sins, one at a time, until we overcome them. We have to do it, of course, but we have all experienced how often our efforts are unsuccessful. Oh, we may actually stop committing the sin, but isn't it true that the *desire* remains in us? No desire is a sin, of course, if we don't choose to have it. Only free choices are sins. But can we say we are fully, perfectly Christian as long as we are simultaneously drawn to and repelled by desires we can't imagine Jesus having? Or his blessed Mother, who was "conceived without sin"?

The problem is not our individual sins or temptations but the fact that we don't have overall the "mind of Christ." To take just one example, how much of our bad behavior is really due to an unrecognized addiction to power? There is no real deliverance until we are wholly transformed into Christ, "transformed by the renewal of our mind"—our whole mind (Romans 12:2; Philippians 2:1–8)—and Christ comes to "full stature" in us (Ephesians 4:13). Our goal is not to be good but to *be Christ*. Wholly. We need to become new wineskins (Matthew 9:17); otherwise, no matter how many holes we plug, new ones will open. Until Christ comes to "full stature" in us, we cry out with Paul, "Who will deliver me?"—not from this particular sin, but "from this body of death" (read Romans 6:1–21).

The truth is, we don't "conquer" sin or "overcome" temptations. Those are words of power. We are *freed* from sin by *surrender* to *Christ in us, the hope of glory*! (Colossians 1:27). When we are wholly in Christ, and he is wholly in us, we will be whole. This is *oneness*—to be whole and entire, undivided, in everything we feel and choose, imagine and embrace, desire and do. This is to *be one* as the Father, Son, and Spirit are one. This is the integrity, the wholeness, the mystery of Christian life. It is to "put on the Lord Jesus Christ" (Romans 13:14).

"He will change our lowly body to conform with his glorified body by the power that enables him also to bring all things into subjection to himself" (Philippians 3:21). That is what we ask for when we pray, *"Your will be done on earth as it is in heaven."* What our religion is all about is letting Christ come to "full stature" in us.

"Your Will Be Done!"

"My Father, if this cannot pass unless I drink it, your will be done."
MATTHEW 26:42

Jesus began his mission as a prophet "teaching in their synagogues, proclaiming the good news of the Kingdom, and curing every disease and sickness" (Matthew 9:35). It was exciting, both for Jesus and for the disciples he "sent ahead of him in pairs to every place where he himself intended to go." They "returned with joy, saying, 'Lord, in your name even the demons submit to us!'" (Matthew 10:1; Luke 10:1). Being a prophet is empowerment. That makes it exciting. In baptism we were empowered and sent as prophets, or "missionary disciples." By bearing witness, we are being different, challenging, accomplishing something. It generates enthusiasm.

But there came a day when Jesus had to be more *priest*—and victim— than prophet. When his "hour had come," Jesus went to "a place called Gethsemane." There he prayed in anguish, "Your will be done." And he begged, "Father, if you are willing, remove this cup from me; yet, not my will but yours be done" (Mark 14:32, 41; Luke 22:39).

A priest offers sacrifice. The sacrifice Jesus offered was his own body. When Matthew first said Jesus "cured all who were sick," he connected this with his passion and death through the *non sequitur*: "This was to fulfill what had been spoken through the prophet Isaiah, 'He took our infirmities and bore our diseases'" (Matthew 8:17; Isaiah

53:4). Jesus' healing miracles prefigured what Peter wrote later: "He himself bore our sins in his body on the cross, so that, free from sins, we might live for righteousness. By his wounds you have been healed" (1 Peter 2:24).

When we pray the words "*Your will be done*," our *dedication to mission* as prophets becomes *surrender to ministry* as "priests in the Priest" and "victims in the Victim." Now we "present our bodies as a living sacrifice to God" (Romans 12:1; John 6:51) so that Jesus might express himself to everyone we meet, "*with us*, *in us*, and *through us*." This requires us to die to our fear of self-exposure and accept the vulnerability of expressing our inmost faith, hope, and love.

To minister we have to mediate the divine life of Jesus to others by giving physical expression to the invisible life of grace within us—without our protecting armor of reserve. To give our "flesh for the life of the world" we must be bread broken and given in the nakedness of uninhibited self-expression, as Jesus was when he hung naked on the cross.

Now we make our own the words Jesus spoke in the garden: "*Your will be done*." We surrender to the ministry of letting Jesus express himself in everything we say and do. This lets him communicate his truth, his love, and his life to everyone we deal with. And it makes us "victims in the Victim." To do this is to die to ourselves in order to live entirely for God and others.

By saying and meaning the words "*Your will be done*" every day, we grow into our baptismal priesthood. This is our fourth step into the mystery and joy of Christian living: from *Christians aware* of living divine lives, to *disciples committed* to reflecting on Christ's words, to *prophets dedicated* to the mission of bearing witness, to *priests surrendered* to ministry. Our religion is a relationship of spousal love: we live to grow into total union of mind, heart, and will with God.

"Here Am I, the Servant of the Lord."

"Be it done to me according to your word." LUKE 1:38

When we "present our bodies as a living sacrifice to God" at baptism, we pray we will "not be conformed to this world, but be transformed by the renewing of our minds." This is so we may "discern what is the will of God—what is good, and acceptable (or pleasing) to God, and perfect" (Romans 12:2). We want to do God's will as perfectly as it is done in heaven.

To keep the Ten Commandments is "good." But for Christians, only the witness of living by Christ's New Law is "acceptable" or "pleasing" to God. To be "perfect," however, we must let Jesus himself act *with us*, *in us*, and *through us* without restraint. This is the *fiat*, the total surrender of Mary: "*Fiat mihi....*Be it done to me according to your word." It is the surrender of Jesus in the garden of Gethsemane: "*Fiat voluntas tua*, your will be done." And this is the *fiat* we make our own in the Our Father: "*Your will be done on earth as it is in heaven.*"

As children of God, we want to live in a way worthy of our Father. So we want the Father's will to be done in us as perfectly as it is in heaven (John 3:5; Luke 3:16; Galatians 5:2). The simplest way to do that is to give ourselves undividedly to others in *ministry* (see Philippians 1:21; 2:4):

> Let each of you look not to your own interests, but to the interests of others. Let the same mind be in you that was in Christ Jesus, who, though he was in the form of God, did not regard equality with God as something to be exploited, but emptied himself, taking the form of a slave, being born in human likeness.

To pray daily, "*Your will be done on earth as it is in heaven,*" is to accept to be the servant of all. This is Christianity: to "let the same mind be in us that was in Christ Jesus" and use the gifts we were given "for the work of ministry, for building up the body of Christ, until we all *become one*" (Ephesians 4:12–13). The fastest way to do this is to "empty" ourselves of status and prestige, which are by nature divisive, and to make sure we are seen and treated as equals and even as the servants of all those we deal with. Even business owners should work, primarily, to serve their families, employees, and fellow members of the human race. That takes precedence over increased and unnecessary profits. (See Pope Francis, *Laudato Si', On Care for Our Common Home*, and *Fratelli Tutti, On Fraternity and Social Friendship*.) In the Church, obviously, priests and bishops should dress and be addressed as servants of their congregations, and any orders they give should be clearly acts of obedience to God who commands them to "feed my sheep" (John 21:15–17). Even the slightest appearance of being "higher" than others smacks of blasphemy, because it makes one look higher than Jesus did on earth (John 13:3–17). Everything in a Christian lifestyle should shout from the housetops: "Here am I, the servant of the Lord."

The truth of Christ's Church is that we are all called to "build up the body of Christ, until we all *become one* in faith!" And the chief means to this unity is surrender to willing, humble service of one another. This shows we are all equally children of the one Father of Jesus who is "over all, works through all, and is in all." Anything that makes anyone appear "higher" than another is inconsistent with the religion of Jesus. We are all equal children of the Father.

Part Five

RESPONSIBILITY FOR CHANGE

"Give us...and forgive us"

"Give Us...and Forgive Us"

I saw the holy city, the new Jerusalem, coming down out of heaven from God, prepared as a bride adorned for her husband.

REVELATION 21:2

The Greek word *epiousion*, which we translate as "daily bread" when we pray "*Give us this day our daily bread*," is not used elsewhere in Scripture and it doesn't really mean "daily." Father Raymond Brown translates it as "future bread," or "the bread of tomorrow," referring to the manna that prefigured the Bread that is Jesus himself. (See his *New Testament Essays*, "The *Pater Noster* as an Eschatological Prayer," and Exodus 16:11–12; John 6:32–58.) The prayer actually says, "*Give us this day the bread that is to come*," asking God to hasten the day when we will all be enjoying together the Bread that is Christ himself at the "wedding banquet of the Lamb."

This requires total mutual forgiveness. The Bread of that banquet is only distributed in a communal meal. There is no takeout, no room service. To partake of that Bread all must accept sitting down together as one family of God, in perfect peace and unity. This means, as Jesus says, that every one of us must forgive our brother or sister from our heart (see Matthew 18:35). So the two petitions, "Give us this day [the Bread of the banquet]," and "Forgive us our sins as we forgive those who sin against us," are one and the same petition. They are inseparable.

And they sum up everything we are asking God to give to us and to the human race. It is the joyous finale of creation and redemption. The "mystery of God's will...God's plan for the fullness of time" is "to sum up all things in Christ, things in heaven and things on earth." In the picture Scripture paints, Christ has "come to full stature." All sins are not just forgiven but "taken away" in the death of the Lamb. Redeemed humanity is "coming down out of heaven from God, prepared as a bride adorned for her husband," a "new creation," innocent, "without a spot or wrinkle or anything of the kind...holy and without blemish." The Father's name is "hallowed" by all. The Kingdom has come. God's will is being done on earth as it is in heaven. And the angel is saying, "Blessed are those who are invited to the marriage supper of the Lamb!" (See Ephesians 1:9; 4:13; 5:27; 2 Corinthians 5:17; Revelation 19:9; 21:2.)

This is the sum of all our desires, the sum of all our prayers. In praying, "*Give us this day the bread that is to come,*" and "*Forgive us our sins as we forgive those who sin against us,*" we abandon ourselves without reserve—all we have and are—to persevering effort to bring every person, area, and activity of human life on earth into unity under the life-giving reign of God, to make the peace and unity of the "wedding banquet" a reality now.

Ultimately it is to live and work for this that we get up in the morning. Taking responsibility for this "with all our heart, with all our soul, with all our mind, and with all our strength" (see Mark 12:30) is the fulfillment of our baptismal consecration as *kings*, or "stewards of the kingship of Christ," living only to bring about God's purpose in creating the world.

> Now to him who by the power at work within us is able
> to accomplish abundantly far more than all we can ask or
> imagine, to him be glory in the Church and in Christ Jesus
> to all generations, forever and ever. Amen. EPHESIANS 3:20–21

The Vision of Peace

There shall be endless peace.... ISAIAH 9:7

When we pray, "*Give us today [or 'this very day'] the bread that is to come*" (Matthew 6:11), we are not asking for what every religion, Christian as well as non-Christian, spontaneously prays for, which is the satisfaction of our daily human needs. "For the kingdom of God is not food and drink but righteousness and peace and joy in the Holy Spirit" (Romans 14:17). Rather, we are asking for what Jesus himself specifically told us to pray for, the purpose for which God created humans, the earth, and everything on it. And that is to "gather together all things in Christ." This mystery is pictured in the image of "the wedding banquet of the Lamb," where all the redeemed are together in perfect peace and harmony around their Father's table, celebrating the union of Jesus with his Bride. This is what our baptismal consecration as "stewards of the kingship of Christ" commits us to work for—already in this world—as the fulfillment of our existence. We must keep this in mind every minute of every day, working constantly to make it the experienced reality of our time. What does that mean in practice?

First, it means we take *responsibility*. For everything. We are never just bystanders, uninvolved onlookers. We are "response-able," answerable to our Father for everything that is happening on earth. It is our duty, our baptismal consecration, to notice anything inconsistent with our Father's will, with the peace and unity of the Kingdom. And then, if we can, to do something about it.

Just to notice is already an initial act of responsibility. What this petition of the Our Father calls us to notice especially is anything that doesn't foster peace and unity. These have to be universal before the "wedding banquet of the Lamb" can take place. Just suppose, for example, that whenever there is disagreement among us, we all gave priority to seeking "unity of spirit, sympathy, love for one another, a tender heart, and a humble mind. Do not repay evil for evil or abuse for abuse; but...seek peace and pursue it" (1 Peter 3:8–11). Suppose every Christian practiced and urged this when divisive or hateful words were spoken. Suppose we argued respectfully for what we believe in without showing contempt for others. Would we, would our country, our world, our politics, be the better for it?

Suppose we accepted the presupposition St. Ignatius of Loyola gives for fruitful dialogue:

> It is necessary to suppose that every good Christian is more ready to put a good interpretation on another's statement than to condemn it as false. If an orthodox construction cannot be put on a proposition, we should ask how the one who made it understands it. If there is error, it should be corrected with all kindness. If this does not suffice, all appropriate means should be used to arrive at a correct interpretation, and so defend the proposition from error.
>
> SEE *SPIRITUAL EXERCISES* 23

What if all social, religious, and political discourse adhered to this, with all sides determined to preserve unity and peace, seeking only that the truth should prevail? What would this do for the common good? Is it something more and more people are seeing as sorely needed today?

"Forgive Us as We Forgive…"

"How often should I forgive? As many as seven times?" MATTHEW 18:21

These words are the first in the Our Father that take notice of anything negative or evil. Jesus has us confront the fact of sin. But his focus is on forgiveness. Whether we are sinning or sinned against, forgiveness is the remedy. Forgiveness is essential to the Father's plan. For us to forgive and be forgiven—entirely, without reserve—is inseparable from the fifth and final goal of our Christian lives—to bring about the universal peace and unity of the wedding banquet of the Lamb.

Note that when we pray, *"Forgive us as we forgive…,"* this differs from, "Have mercy on me, a sinner." It is universal reconciliation. It addresses the sin and evil of the whole world, of all creation. In fact, the spousal love we prayed for earlier is also universal. While on earth spousal love is by nature exclusive, one on one; in heaven, when the restrictions of time and space no longer apply, spousal love is communal. The difference is that spousal love on earth is essentially a commitment to strive for union, but in heaven that union is a mystery already realized. We will all be one in Christ the Bridegroom and in the Church his Bride, one as the Three Persons of the Trinity are one. Jesus prayed that we all may be one: "as you, Father, are in me and I am in you, may they also be in us" (John 17:21). That is the mystery of heaven.

As St. Augustine said, in heaven, "There will be but one Christ, loving himself."

This love is based on mercy and forgiveness, for they are the only answer to evil. They alone can heal the divisions brought about by sin. The reason God is so demanding about universal forgiveness is that without it there can be no "wedding banquet of the Lamb," and the goal of creation itself cannot be realized. So the Father first empowers us, then requires us, like himself, to forgive everyone, totally and without exception, beginning now.

We don't deny this can take time. Jesus taught as much in the parable of the "mustard seed that a man took and planted in his garden. When it was fully grown, it became a large bush and the birds of the sky dwelt in its branches." He said, "The Kingdom of God...is like yeast that a woman took and mixed in with three measures of wheat flour until the whole batch of dough was leavened" (Luke 13:18–21). To be faithful stewards we have to be willing to wait—as we say in the Mass, "We await the blessed hope and the coming of our Savior, Jesus Christ."

But we can begin now by forgiving everyone who has ever sinned against us. We cannot take our place at the wedding banquet of the Lamb until we do, so why not begin now to bring about the peace and unity of the Kingdom? Why let God's desire for all creation be blocked by us?

The words *"Forgive us as we forgive..."* are both a prayer and a promise. As we make the prayer, God will help us grow into the promise. But we have to do our part.

That is our religion: to work for "the peace and unity of the Kingdom." We find our own good in working for the good of all. Another word for this is "love."

Part Six

ABANDONMENT TO DEATH

Subject Us Not to the Trial / Let Us Not Pass through Hard Testing

"Subject us not..."

God is faithful, and he will not let you be tested beyond your strength.

1 CORINTHIANS 10:13

"*Lead us not into temptation*" is another poor translation. A better one is "*Subject us not to the trial*" (New Zealand bishops), or "*Let us not pass through hard testing*" (based on Raymond Brown).

On May 22, 2019, Pope Francis approved a change in these words for liturgical use. He had said earlier that the current translation implies God leads people into temptation, an action that is against his nature as a good and holy God. "A father doesn't do that," Francis said. "A father helps you get up immediately. It's Satan who leads us into temptation; that's his department."

Father Raymond Brown says the "trial" the Scripture text actually refers to is the cosmic one thought to precede the end of the world, "the final battle between God and Satan" referred to in Revelation 3:10: "I will keep you from the hour of trial that is coming on the whole world to test the inhabitants of the earth." But the point of the whole Book of Revelation is that Jesus wins, so we should live in hope rather than fear. Christians know this, and it is our duty, our mission, to make it known to others. That is why we celebrate the resurrection, Christ's and our own.

It is legitimate to apply to our own death what is said about the trial that precedes the end of the world. For each one of us, death is our personal end of the world. Just as Christian devotion—inaccurately but permissibly—converted "the bread that is to come" into "daily bread" to refer to our daily needs, so we can make the petition *Subject us not to the trial* a plea for perseverance in our daily trials, and especially for final perseverance "at the hour of our death," for which we also pray in the Hail Mary. This is a reassuring way to begin our day. If Jesus himself teaches us to ask the Father to keep us from being tested beyond our strength, then we have every reason to believe the Father will do that for us—not only at the hour of our death, but all day, every day. St. Paul affirms this: "God is faithful, and he will not let you be tested beyond your strength" (1 Corinthians 10:13).

For Christians, death is a culmination, a graduation, a reward, the achievement of what we have been living and working for all our lives, our final and complete surrender to God in love. It doesn't destroy life; it brings the life we have been living to completion (1 Corinthians 15:53–55):

> For this perishable body must put on imperishability, this mortal body immortality....Then the saying will be fulfilled: "Death has been swallowed up in victory. Where, O death, is your victory? Where, O death, is your sting?"

Death is the greatest free moment of life, because it is the moment when we make the greatest free choice of our lives. Saying yes to death is the all-inclusive, irrevocable choice to bestow ourselves on God without reserve—definitively and forever. That is why it is the fulfillment of the "first and greatest" commandment: "You shall love the Lord your God with *all* your heart, and with *all* your soul, and with *all* your mind, and with *all* your strength" (Mark 12:30; Matthew 22:38; Deuteronomy 6:5). Because Christianity is a religion of hope and joy, there is more anticipation than apprehension in the words *"Subject us not to the trial!"* To fear death is against our religion.

Help against Hard Testing

Are any among you sick?...Pray over them, anointing them with oil.
JAMES 5:14

Faith, hope, and love are seldom pure in our actual experience of life. We act with mixed motives, guided by human reason as well as faith. Often, we do what Jesus teaches because it "makes sense" for human fulfillment as well as divine. Here nature and grace cooperate.

But some decisions are inspired by truth known only by divine faith and motivated only by divine hope and love. Then grace is calling us to go beyond what is natural to us and to act on the level of God. The decision to accept death is the last and most inclusive of those decisions.

That is why Fr. Karl Rahner, SJ, called death "the greatest free moment of life." It is also the most challenging, because to choose death we have to be completely "purified" of dependence on our natural guidance system and act totally by divine faith, hope, and love. If we don't work at this during life, consciously trying to grow in living the life of grace, then at death we will have some catching up to do. This is the result of neglecting that "asceticism," spiritual training, that Rahner calls "an exercise in Christian death." Every parish pastoral plan should address this.

Before we can willingly say yes to death we have to "let go" of any restrictive dependence on the sense of security we get on earth from being alive and well. If we have neglected that "exercise in Christian death" that prepares us to surrender our lives to God with confidence, we will find that yes a hard word to pronounce. And we will hang between heaven and earth, so to speak, until we say it. That is why we pray, "*Let us not pass through hard testing.*"

But at that moment, the Church teaches, the prayers of others can help us. When we are struggling to say, "Yes, Father, into your hands I commend my spirit," whether before or after we are medically dead (we are not really dead until God says so), the prayers of all who have prayed, are praying, or will pray for us when they learn of our death will be present to us at that moment, supporting us and encouraging us to believe, to hope, to love without reserve.

This may be why the oil for the sacrament of the sick is blessed at a special Chrism Mass celebrated by priests and laity representing all the parishes in the diocese, gathered together with the bishop. This makes the whole diocese present in symbol and in truth whenever that oil is used. So if we are dying when we receive the sacrament, we should be aware that everyone in the diocese—in the whole Church, really—is gathered around us, reinforcing our faith with their own, saying, "*Proficisere, anima Christiana de hoc mundo!* Go forth upon your journey, Christian soul! Go in peace! Let go! Go to God!" (See Newman's oratorio, *Dream of Gerontius.*) The faith, the hope, the love of the whole Church will be bolstering ours. And our Father will be saving us from "hard testing."

We pray for this in every Our Father when we ask, *"Subject us not to the trial. Let us not pass through hard testing."* For Christians who try all their lives to live consciously by faith, hope, and love, saying yes to death will not be very new. Our religion is a constant yes to death.

"Deliver Us from Evil"

"Do not be afraid, little flock, for it is your Father's good pleasure to give you the kingdom." LUKE 12:32

Father Raymond Brown joins this petition to the previous one, and points out that, while the Western Church prefers "Deliver us from evil," meaning evil in general, the Greek Church prays, "Deliver us from the evil one," meaning Satan, which he supports as the better translation.

We can profit from both. It is good to remind ourselves there is a real live enemy out there, the devil, trying to deceive and mislead us. Scripture says, "Keep alert. Like a roaring lion, your adversary the devil prowls around, looking for someone to devour" (1 Peter 5:8). The whole art of "discernment of spirits" is based on recognition of this, as is the "Awareness Exercise" when used as a form of daily prayer (see above, "How to Use Our Feelings," page 29). Although we do not attribute every misleading interior inclination specifically to the devil, we allow for the possibility. And it helps if we are aware of his tactics.

St. Ignatius of Loyola pinpointed the general strategy of Satan in the "Two Standards" meditation of his *Spiritual Exercises*, no. 142: "First they are to tempt people to covet riches, that they may the more easily attain the empty honors of this world, and then come to overweening pride. The first step, then, will be riches, the second honors, the third pride. From these three steps the evil one leads to all other vices." This explains why people who know this strategy, like Pope Francis, try to live simply and shun pompous titles and protocol. It is spiritual self-defense.

This phrase of the Our Father also reminds us that we can count on God to deliver us from every evil. Jesus said, "Do not fear....Not a sparrow falls to the ground without your Father's consent. Even the hairs of your head are all counted. So do not be afraid; you are of more value than many sparrows" (see Matthew 10:28ff.).

The faith we profess is in "God the Father Almighty, Creator of heaven and earth." As such, God has control over "all things, visible and invisible." God can and will deliver us from all evil. If God permits anything to happen that we perceive as evil, we know God can keep it from harming us, and even make it work for our good (Luke 21:16–19; Romans 8:28).

Praying, "*Deliver us from evil,*" lets us begin our day conscious of the happy ending that this day and every day will have when, on the "day of the Lord," Jesus comes again in glory to "present the Church to himself in splendor, without a spot or wrinkle or anything of the kind—yes, so that she may be holy and without blemish" (Ephesians 5:27). Then Christ will reign forever and ever.

That is what we look forward to, and what we trust in, when we pray, "*Deliver us from evil.*" If we pray this consistently every morning when we wake up, then all day long we will be able to deal with everything we think, feel, and confront from a position of security and hope.

"*Do not be afraid*" is a fundamental principle of our religion. That is something to live by.

The Bedrock Benefits of Christianity

The breadth and length and height and depth, and to know the love of Christ that surpasses knowledge. EPHESIANS 3:18–19

All beings have four things in common: *Being*, *Truth*, *Goodness*, and *Oneness*. These are the bedrock characteristics of everything that is. By telling us God loves us enough to share God's own divine self with us on these deepest levels of existence, the Our Father proclaims the "breadth and length and height and depth" of Christ's love so that we may be "filled with all the fullness of God" (Ephesians 3:18–19). And that is what the Christian life is all about.

In living beings, *Being* is synonymous with *Life*. Jesus said, "I came that they might have life and have it abundantly"—that is, the fullness of God's own divine life (John 10:10). The first words of the Our Father make us aware of this promise by calling God *"Our Father, who art in heaven."*

All beings have *Truth*, intelligibility. Jesus has shared, not just some truths, but the divine Truth of God: "All that I have learned from the Father, I have made known to you" (John 15:15). We celebrate this promise and commit ourselves as disciples to pursue this Truth when we pray, *"Hallowed be your name."* We can pursue it because it is promised.

All beings are *Good*. The good we desire becomes our goal in life. When Jesus announces, "The kingdom of God has come near; repent [*metanoiete*, change your goal in life] and believe in the Good News" (Mark 1:15), he is sharing with us the deepest Good there is: divine Goodness. When we pray *"Your kingdom come!"* we accept this new Good for ourselves and dedicate ourselves to the mission of proclaiming it to all humanity. We become like God.

We identify something as *One*—as a single being—when we see that all its parts are ordered to work together for a common end. When Jesus taught us to pray, "*Your will be done*," he called—and enabled—us to surrender to doing the will of the Father as perfectly "*on earth as it is in heaven.*" This calls us to a oneness of mind and will and heart with God that is divine. Jesus himself prayed, "That they may all be one. As you, Father, are in me and I am in you, may they also be in us" (John 17:21). This is the unity of God.

When we realize God loves us enough to share with us everything God is on these deepest levels of existence, we know what Christianity is. It is being one with God in the four bedrock areas of human existence. That is what this book has been all about.

Review

WHAT WE CAN LOOK BACK ON SO FAR...

In teaching us to pray, "*Father*," Jesus calls us to an openness of mind that accepts divine truth, mystery beyond our human comprehension. This is life-enhancing. It removes the spiritual myopia that keeps us from seeing that, as *Christians*, we share in the infinite *Being*, *Truth*, *Goodness*, and *Oneness* that constitute the Life of God. Jesus tells us to relate to God as family members—not primarily as "Lord God, heavenly King," or "Almighty God," but as "Father" (see the Gloria). Our first focus should not be on adoration, or even praise and thanksgiving, but on *relationship*. We are sons and daughters of the Father. We share God's own divine life. We are divine.

In teaching us to pray, "*Our* Father," Jesus tells us that relationship with other human beings is a constitutive element of our relationship with him. There is no purely one-on-one spirituality, relationship with God, or beatitude. We live and deal with God, in this life and the next, as members both of the human community and of the divine-human community of God's children.

In teaching us to pray, "Our Father *who art in heaven*," Jesus tells us we are not just residents of this planet but that our "citizenship is in heaven" (Philippians 3:20). As sharers in the *Being* of God, we have Life eternal. We are also empowered and called to live now on the level of God. Therefore, we must "not be conformed to this world, but transformed by the renewing of our minds, so that we may discern what is the will of God—what is good and acceptable and perfect" (Romans 12:2).

In teaching us to pray, *"Hallowed be your name,"* Jesus calls us to enter fully into the gift of *faith*, which is a sharing in God's own act of knowing divine *Truth*. He tells us we are invited into a personal relationship—into deep, personal friendship—with God. We are called to keep trying to know God better so that we can make God better known by others.

In teaching us to pray, *"Your Kingdom come,"* Jesus calls us to enter fully into the gift of *hope*, the gift of living for the *Good* God promises. We are able and willing to base our life visibly on God's promises because by hope we share in God's own act of intending to fulfill them. Here Jesus tells us we have been chosen, selected, as Christ's coworkers, to continue Christ's own mission as *prophets* to proclaim the divine *Good* of the Kingdom of God on earth.

In teaching us to pray, *"Your will be done on earth as it is in heaven,"* Jesus switches our focus from *what* to *who*, from bringing about good results in the world to entering fully into the union of *spousal love* with God. He invites us into that perfect *Oneness* of mind and will and heart that is the only way the Father's will can be done as perfectly on earth as it is in heaven. This is surrender to ministry as *priests* who in all our words and actions make visible the self-expression of God in us and through us.

In teaching us to pray, *"Give us...and forgive us,"* Jesus calls us to take responsibility for uniting the whole human race with God and with each other in perfect union of mind and will and heart. This was God's ultimate purpose in creating the world. Jesus presents this in the image of the "wedding banquet of the Lamb," where the "bread" that gives joy is Jesus himself, and the only way to partake of the Bread is to sit down as *one* with all the redeemed in a communal meal that presupposes total mutual acceptance and forgiveness. As *stewards* of Christ's kingship, we live to bring about this peace and unity on earth.

In teaching us to pray, "*Subject us not to the trial,*" Jesus calls us to bear witness to the resurrection—Christ's and ours—by the way we live and the way we die. Our whole life should be a preparation for Christian death. When we say, "Yes! Father, into your hands I commend my spirit," it is the greatest free moment of life, the moment when our faith, hope, and love come to perfection.

WHAT COMES NEXT?

At this point we have a basic understanding—a theological under-standing—of the mysteries of the Our Father. We have not fully absorbed any of them, because we will keep doing that all our lives. But now every morning we can let the meaning, the taste, and the tone of each word slowly settle into our hearts as we give to the rec-itation of the Our Father whatever amount of time we choose. As we grow in understanding and appreciation, the words of the prayer Jesus taught will gradually transform our lives.

Our Father will help us accept that we are
called to live divine lives as *Christians*.

Hallowed be your name! will assure us we can know God
if we commit to be *disciples*.

Your Kingdom come! will strengthen our dedication to mission
as *prophets*.

*Your will be done...*will motivate total surrender
to God in ministry as *priests*.

*Give us...and forgive us...*will keep us focused on
bringing about the unity and peace for which we take
responsibility as *stewards* of the kingship of Christ.

Let us not pass through hard testing will keep us looking forward
to the greatest free moment of life, when we say, "Yes! Father, into
your hands I commend my spirit," with total faith, hope, and love.

If we wish, we can take time during or outside of morning prayer to meditate on the Our Father according to the complete "Second Method of Prayer" St. Ignatius teaches (*Spiritual Exercises* 250–57). We do this by "meditating upon each word as long as we find various meanings, comparisons, relish, and consolation in the consideration of it...and not be anxious to go on, though the whole time be taken up with what we have found. When the time is over, we can finish by saying the rest of the Our Father in the usual way."

What I have written above is the fruit of many hours spent reflecting and writing on the words of the Our Father. Now, when I recite them slowly during morning prayer, I can savor them with greater understanding and appreciation. This is the blessing God bestows on everyone who devotes time to the prayer that Jesus himself taught us to pray. May that blessing be yours!

APPENDIX

This book has been a series of commentaries and reflections on the Our Father to help us learn to pray what we say.

But in the introduction, I said it would sum up everything I have learned about what it means to live as a Christian and that everything essential is already summarized in the prayer taught by Jesus himself, the Our Father. Now I would like to show in a systematic way how it does that.

For catechists, DREs, those involved in the RCIA or just in sacramental preparation, such an explanation can be of great help. My goal is to show how everything boils down to six essential doctrines and practices that are the six themes and parts of this book. They present:

1. the six basic *mysteries and joys* of Christianity;
2. the six *objectives or duties* intrinsic to Christian living that we must not (but frequently do) overlook;
3. the six *practical concerns* of which we should be conscious as we live our daily lives;
4. the six *pastoral goals* that should be explicit in parish and diocesan ministry.

By pointing out how these four elements appear in all six themes of the book, this appendix shows readers what to look for and notice in each part of the book and helps them apply to their daily living what they read in each chapter.

But there is more. The appendix also shows that these six themes are so incorporated into basic Christian living that we cannot ignore any one of them and still claim to live a complete, authentic Christian life. It does this by pointing out how they include, and are included, in all the common operations of Christian living: the *sacraments*, the *liturgy* (Mass), and the exercise of the *"theological virtues"* of divine Faith, Hope, and Love. They show up everywhere.

They are also inherent in four areas less known outside of philosophical circles but nevertheless fundamental to understanding Christian existence: the four "Transcendentals of Being." These are the four bedrock attributes common to everything that exists, "transcending" all differences, even between finite and infinite existence. The four "Transcendentals" are:

Being (in living beings synonymous with *Life*),
Truth,
Goodness,
and *Oneness.*

The appendix shows how these "Transcendental" elements of existence come into focus in the six parts or themes of this book. This assures us we are dealing here with the rock-bottom realities of Christian existence.

All of this supports the claim that these six themes, mysteries, experiences, and commitments are the six essential elements of an authentic Christian life.

Part One: Awareness of Relationship

Our Father who art in heaven

"Our Father": The first thing the prayer of Jesus tells us is that we should call God "Father." To be *Christian* is to accept the *new relationship* with God that makes us divine.

The first, most basic *mystery and joy* of Christianity is that we share in the divine life of God as true children of the Father. By "the grace of the Lord Jesus Christ," we are empowered and called to live divine lives. And this is not earned but given free—to everyone reborn by sharing in the death and resurrection of Jesus.

Our first *objective, duty, and priority* in life must always be to glorify God. But to do that, the first thing we need to be taught and learn as Christians is to accept and live out our *divine identity* as Christians. Only with this awareness can we glorify God as we should.

So in practice, our first *practical concern* should be to live consciously as Christians by cultivating constant *awareness* of the divine mystery of our being. And our first *pastoral goal and priority* as Church should be to announce and teach this to everyone so all will know how to glorify God as they should. This is why Jesus has us pray, "*Our Father.*"

We also need to recognize divine identity in others. This includes giving the benefit of the doubt to those we assume to be, without their knowing it, "anonymous Christians" through "baptism of desire" (see the *Catechism of the Catholic Church*, 1260, 1281).

Christianity is a religion of mystery, of divine identity through relationship with God.

We find this first theme:

- *In the sacraments:* our first theme explains "grace"—that is, the "favor of sharing in God's divine life"—which is the essence of what *baptism* gives (Romans 6:3–11).
- *In the liturgy:* the Church announces and celebrates our first theme, divine identity, in the Introductory Rites of every Mass (from the Sign of the Cross and Greeting to the Opening Prayer). Being aware of this will add to our appreciation of Mass.
- *In all three of the "theological virtues"* of divine Faith, Hope, and Love.

- *In the "Transcendental" of Being* (in living beings synonymous with *Life*), which comes into focus here because God's identity and ours is a mystery of Life, human and divine.

Part Two: Commitment to Discipleship

Hallowed be your name

To pray, "*Hallowed be your name!*" is to accept the invitation to enter into personal relationship and friendship with God through committed *discipleship*. This is the second basic *mystery and joy* of Christianity.

Once we have accepted our divine identity, the words "*Hallowed be your name!*" tell us our second practical *objective and duty* is to work at making God known and loved. Obviously, in order to make God known to others, we first have to know God intimately ourselves, and this should be our second *practical concern*.

Our second *pastoral concern* as Church, then, should be to urge and teach all the baptized to be *disciples*. To be disciples of Jesus—the word means "students"—requires *commitment* to studying the words that reveal his heart. This is a commitment to the three Rs of *reading* (a form of *remembering*), *reflecting* on, and *responding* to the words of God.

"*Hallowed be your name!*" tells us Jesus came to make the Father's "name," God's person, known and loved by everyone. That was his first *priority*, the first thing Jesus himself prayed for and taught us to ask for in our prayer: "*Father, hallowed be your name!*"

That is also how Jesus summed up his work: "I have made your name known to those whom you gave me from the world." Jesus said he came that we might "have life, and have it abundantly," which we find in knowing the Father: "This is eternal life, that they may *know you*, the only true God, and Jesus Christ whom you have sent" (John 10:10; 17:3).

In teaching us to pray, *"Hallowed be your name,"* Jesus tells us we are invited into personal relationship, into intimate friendship, with God. That makes Christianity a religion of mystical experience. When we know God as revealed by Jesus Christ, our religion is authentic. Then we are entering into the fullness of life.

We find this second theme:

- *In the sacrament of reconciliation:* if we use it as we should, it helps us grow into the mind and heart of God by constantly reforming our thoughts, words, and actions. This is discipleship.
- *In the liturgy:* the *General Instruction on the Roman Missal,* 2002, says the purpose of the Liturgy of the Word at Mass is to "promote meditation" on God's word, which makes us disciples, "students" of God's mind and will and heart.
- *In the "theological virtue"* of divine *Faith,* by which we understand divine *Truth.*
- *In the "Transcendental"* of *Truth,* which comes into focus here because God's word is the revelation of divine *Truth.*

Part Three: Dedication to Mission

"Your Kingdom come"

When baptizing, immediately after pouring the water, the minister anoints the new Christian with chrism, saying God the Father "anoints you with the Chrism of salvation, so that you may remain members of Christ, Priest, Prophet and King, unto eternal life."

The third basic *mystery and joy* of Christian living is that we have been selected to carry on the messianic mission of Jesus as Prophet, Priest, and King. These three words give us our job description as Christians. When we pray *"Your Kingdom come!"* we are expressing our dedication to that mission.

This means our third *objective and duty* as Christians, after keeping ourselves aware of our *divine identity* and committing ourselves to grow into it through *discipleship*, is to carry out our mission as *prophets*. We dedicate ourselves to *evangelize* (announce the Good News) through *witness*. This should be our third *practical concern* as Christians.

So our third *pastoral priority* as Church should be to urge and encourage all the baptized to live out their baptismal consecration as prophets by dedicating themselves to the *mission* of proclaiming the Good News. Primarily this means bearing *witness* to the gospel through a *lifestyle* that cannot be explained without it. This is, and should be taught as, the third essential of Christian life.

This implies a commitment to *continual conversion* and *change*. Christianity is not a stagnant religion. If the Church today looked like it did a century ago, that would mean the mustard seed has died (see Matthew 13:31–32). And if our own way of living the faith—our attitudes, values, and lifestyle—is not constantly changing, we are not completely alive.

Our religion might be demanding, but no one can say it is boring. Jesus came to "make all things new" (see Mark 2:22; Revelation 21:5). He is still doing it. Through us.

We find this third theme:
- *In the sacrament of confirmation*: when we reaffirm our dedication to mission as adults, and the bishop "confirms" the Church's recognition of our baptism.

- *In the presentation of gifts at Mass*, when we place bread and wine on the altar as symbols of ourselves, who are also the "fruit of the earth and work of human hands" (we form ourselves by our choices to be the unique persons we are), to be empowered and used as creatures to do God's divine work. This renews our dedication to mission.
- *In the "theological virtue"* of divine *Hope*, which lets us pursue the humanly unattainable Good of the Kingdom.
- *In the "Transcendental"* of *Goodness*, which comes into focus here because the Kingdom is divine *Goodness* embodied in human life.

Part Four: Surrender to Ministry

"Your will be done on earth as it is in heaven"

When we pray *"Your will be done on earth as it is in heaven!"* we surrender ourselves to the constant *ministry* of letting the Father, Son, and Spirit express God's true self:

- in and through all our physical words and actions
- to everyone we deal with
- in order to give or enhance divine life in them

Doing this presupposes deep union of mind and will and heart with God. And the pledge to work toward this intimate relationship and total surrender is what defines *spousal love*.

This is the fourth basic *mystery and joy* of Christian living: we are chosen to carry on the mission of Jesus as *priests in the Priest* and *victims in the Victim*. To do this we "present our bodies as a living sacrifice, holy and acceptable to God" (see Romans 12:1).

So, after accepting to live divine lives as reborn children of Our Father, to "*hallow*" the Father's name as *disciples*, and to announce the *Kingdom of God* as *prophets*, our fourth *personal objective*, *concern*, and *pastoral priority* should be to live out, and encourage all the baptized to live out, our baptismal consecration as *priests*. We do this by embracing the *ministry* of surrendering to God's expression of divine *Life*, *Truth*, *Goodness*, and unifying *Love* with us, in us, and through us in all our interactions with every person we deal with.

Because our self-expression is physical and human, we speak of this surrender as a relationship of identification with God incarnate in Jesus. It is like the union of body members with their head, or of branches with the vine. We are not just coworkers or messengers "sent." We make the sender, Father, Son, and Spirit, present by "being Christ," making Jesus present as expressing himself physically here and now, in and through our bodies, as we ask him to do in the prayer: "Lord, do this *with me*; do this *in me*; do this *through me*."

We find this fourth theme:
- *In the sacraments* of *matrimony* and *holy orders* in which we surrender our "flesh for the life of the world" through life-giving love and ministry (see John 6:51). To give and to nurture life as we should, both physically and spiritually, we surrender to the total sharing of spousal love with God and, if married, with each other.
- *In the eucharistic prayer at Mass*, when we say, with and in Christ "lifted up" at the consecration, "This is *my body*, given up for you," *my flesh* for the life of the world.
- *In the "theological virtue"* of *Love*, of which this unity is the highest experience.
- *In the "Transcendental"* of *Oneness*, which comes into focus here because this union with God is like the divine *Oneness* of

the Three Persons with each other and with us in the Church: a mystery we are called to express, experience, and probe.

Part Five: Responsibility for Change

"Give us…and forgive us"

The fifth basic *mystery and joy* of Christian living is this: God has revealed to us not only where we come from but where we are going, and our responsibility for getting the whole world there. We know God's goal, God's desire and plan for all creation. And through our baptismal consecration as "kings," or "administrators" of Christ's kingship, God has entrusted us with responsibility for realizing it, as much as possible, already on earth.

So our fifth *personal objective, concern*, and *pastoral goal* should be to *take responsibility* ourselves and urge others to take responsibility for bringing about *change* in the world in order to realize "the mystery of God's will, his plan for the fullness of times," to gather together, sum up in Christ as head, everything in heaven and on earth (Ephesians 1:9–10).

God explains this in Scripture, using the image of "the wedding banquet of the Lamb" (Revelation 19:9). In heaven all the redeemed are seated together in perfect peace and harmony around their Father's table, celebrating the marriage of Jesus to his Bride, the Church. This image inspires us to desire completely and uniquely the goal of creation: the *"wedding banquet of the Lamb."* We have turned over to God all that we have and are. Now we use it all to *work with persevering hope* to bring every area and activity of human life into peace and unity under the life-giving reign of Christ.

This is the true meaning of the words "*Give us this day the bread that is to come* [not *our daily bread*], *and forgive us our sins as we forgive those who sin against us.*"

We find this fifth theme:
- *In the sacrament* of *anointing of the sick*, given to strengthen us for our total yes to God at death, which is also a standing pledge of support whenever we need it during life.
- *In the rite of Communion at Mass*, when we celebrate Christ's final victory and "the wedding banquet of the Lamb." Notice the focus on "peace" and "unity."
- *In the "theological virtue"* of *Love*, because embracing this responsibility is an experience of sharing the total, universal, divine Love Jesus revealed when he took on the responsibility of inviting and preparing the whole human race for the "wedding banquet of the Lamb."
- *In the "Transcendental"* of *Oneness* again, which comes into focus here because to understand this goal is to understand the mystery of the divine Oneness of all creation, and especially of redeemed humans, called to be One as the Father, Son, and Spirit are One (John 17:22).

Part Six: Abandonment to Death

Subject us not to the trial /
Let us not pass through hard testing

The sixth basic *mystery and joy* of Christian living is abandonment to death for the sake of *resurrection* to eternal life, a central theme of Christian evangelization. The word *resurrection* appears forty times in the New Testament, 102 if we count the times Jesus is described as "risen" or "raised." "Eternal life" appears forty-four times, and only in the New Testament.

Abandonment to death is the "gift of final perseverance." The words *"Subject us not to the trial"*—a more accurate translation than the misleading *"Lead us not into temptation"*—ask God to make it easier for us to say, "Yes! Father, into your hands I commend my spirit," when it is time to go to God (Luke 23:46). Our final act of Christian witness on earth, and our sixth *objective* and *concern* as Christians, is to bear witness to the whole world by the way we live and by the way we die, that for us the words "death" and "resurrection" are inseparable. A Christian death should be characterized by the same "fruit of the spirit" that we should manifest throughout our lives: "love, joy, peace, patient endurance, kindness, generosity, faithfulness, gentleness, and [the] self-control [of total surrender to God]" (Galatians 5:22–23). We should live visibly in the anticipated joy of eternal life. Christians should be known as those who are always aware that Jesus said: "This is the will of my Father, that all who see the Son and believe in him may have eternal life; and I will raise them up on the last day" (John 6:40).

Our sixth *pastoral concern* should be to teach people to prepare for a "happy death"—with the joy of those "invited to the marriage supper of the Lamb." Instead of hearing Christ's words just as warnings to be sure we are not in mortal sin when we die, we should let them inspire us to make our whole life a preparation for death (compare Matthew, chapters 23–25 and Philippians 2:12 with 1 Corinthians 2:9; Revelation 19:9; 1 John 3:2). We do this by "seeking perfection," working daily at letting "the same mind be in us that was in Christ Jesus," so we won't have so much adjusting to do when he is fully revealed. Then "we will be like him, for we will see him as he is." Aware of this, we start becoming now what we know we will have to be to "fit in" where we will live forever after death.

Christianity is an ongoing experience of joyful anticipation, waiting for "the blessed hope and the manifestation of the glory" of "Christ in us, the hope of glory" (Titus 2:13; Colossians 1:27). Jesus came "so that my joy may be in you, and your joy may be complete" (John 15:11). The words "*Subject us not to the trial*" motivate us to seek that joy.

We find this sixth theme:

- *In the sacrament* of *anointing of the sick*, which helps us say our total yes to God.
- *In the rite of Communion at Mass*, which celebrates Christ's victory over sin and death.
- *In the "theological virtues"* of *Faith*, *Hope*, and *Love*. This is the culmination of them all.
- *In all four "Transcendentals"* of *Being*, *Truth*, *Goodness* and *Oneness*, because our yes to death is our ultimate acceptance of the bedrock realities of our divine existence.

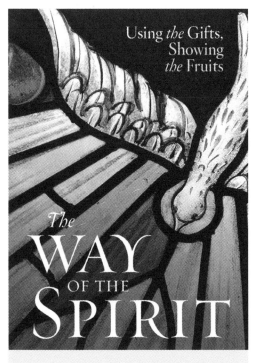

In this powerful book, Fr. David Knight fervently reminds us that to live a Christian life means actively embracing the gifts of the Holy Spirit. Here, he shows how infusing our daily lives with wisdom, understanding, knowledge, and counsel along with family spirit, strength, and awe of the Lord will bear fruit in our relationships and our spiritual and emotional health. A must-read for everyone committed to the way of Christ, this book, Fr. Knight says, can "be a new beginning for you to live life to the fullest."

144 PAGES | **$16.95** | **5½" X 8½"** | **ORDER 855976** | **978-1-62785-597-6**

TO ORDER CALL 1-800-321-0411
OR VISIT WWW.TWENTYTHIRDPUBLICATIONS.COM

TWENTY-THIRD PUBLICATIONS
A division of Bayard, Inc.